The Law Commission
Consultation Paper No. 126

Administrative Law:
Judicial Review and Statutory Appeals

LONDON: HMSO

THE LAW COMMISSION

ADMINISTRATIVE LAW:

JUDICIAL REVIEW AND STATUTORY APPEALS

TABLE OF CONTENTS

ADMINISTRATIVE LAW: JUDICIAL REVIEW AND STATUTORY APPEALS

1   **INTRODUCTION**

1.1   Under item 10 of our Fifth Programme of Law Reform[1] we are undertaking an
           examination of the procedures and forms of relief available by way of judicial
           review and those governing statutory appeals and applications to the High Court
           from the decisions of inferior courts, tribunals and other bodies. Our 1976 Report
           on Remedies in Administrative Law[2] paved the way for the modern procedure in
           R.S.C., Order 53. The main focus of the present exercise will be on the
           effectiveness of the procedural mechanisms put in place in 1977 and revised in
           1980.[3] We have, in particular, undertaken to consider several areas known to be
           problematical, but this is not to be seen as limiting the generality of our remit.
           Our programme consciously chose not to look at the substantive grounds for
           judicial review, which we believe should be the subject of judicial development.
           We propose to consider and make recommendations, which will ensure that
           continuing development of the grounds for review is facilitated by the procedural
           framework.

1.2   There have been many calls for further reform in this field including those from
           the Committee of the JUSTICE-All Souls Review of Administrative Law[4] and
           Lord Woolf,[5] notably his Hamlyn lectures in 1989. The understanding of this
           branch of administrative law and the issues provoking the need for reform has been
           enhanced by the increase of case-law and academic commentary, in particular the
           contribution of Professor Sir William Wade Q.C..

1.3   Even before we embarked on our research, we were aware of the wide interest
           which our further examination of this area of the law would provoke and this has
           guided the manner in which we intend to seek views on the scope for reform. We
           publicised the fact of our review widely and we have actively encouraged those

---

[1]   (1991) Law Com. No. 200.

[2]   Report on Remedies in Administrative Law, Law Com. No. 73.

[3]   S.I. 1977, No. 1955; S.I. 1980, No. 2000. See also Supreme Court Act 1981, s.
           31.

[4]   *Administrative Justice: Some Necessary Reforms* (1988).

[5]   *Protection of the Public - A New Challenge* (1990) (hereafter *"Hamlyn lectures"*),
           and "Judicial Review: A Possible Programme for Reform", [1992] P.L. 221. See
           also "A Hotchpotch of Appeals - the Need for a Blender" (1988), 7 C.J.Q. 44.

who have direct involvement with the procedure for judicial review to bring particular issues to our attention. Our plan is to allow a generous period for public consultation on this paper, and to follow up during the consultation period some of the most significant points raised by those who have approached us on specific matters. We understand that the Public Law Project, in conjunction with Maurice Sunkin of the University of Essex, is conducting empirical research on access to and the use of judicial review with the support of the Nuffield Foundation and that two preliminary reports on the findings should be published in early 1993. One will analyse the processing and results of all applications for judicial review lodged in the Crown Office between 1987 and 1989 and in the first quarter of 1991, including decisions on leave and at substantive hearings, the extent of withdrawals, and patterns of use in different subject areas. The second will examine the availability of legal aid for judicial review.[6]

1.4 It is inevitably the case that some of the points which have been raised are so specific to a particular context that they are not appropriate to be covered in this paper. We cannot dwell in detail on all the points which are problematical, but we invite views on points which we have not been able to discuss fully. As ever, we emphasise that this paper forms just the start of the public consultative process; any views contained in this paper are only *provisional* and they are included because we know from experience that consultees find it helpful to react to specific suggestions. After the consultation period is concluded, we shall analyse the views put to us and then consider our final recommendations.

1.5 This paper does not consider whether public authorities should be liable to compensate those injured by invalid administrative action, although the matter is touched on in the section on interim relief.[7] The fact that English law does not provide for such compensation has long been the subject of criticism,[8] and a number of factors, including developments in European Community law,[9] suggest that the availability of compensation against public authorities requires reconsideration. However, whether compensation should be available and, if so, what its scope should be calls for deeper study than we could conveniently give it in the present paper.

---

[6] Copies of these reports will be available from the Public Law Project, Room 505, Charles Clore House, Institute of Advanced Legal Studies, 17 Russell Sq., London WC1B 5DR.

[7] See paras. 6.13 and 6.15 below.

[8] For recent examples (although taking different approaches) see the JUSTICE-All Souls Report, *op. cit.*, ch. 11; Woolf, *Hamlyn Lectures*, pp. 56-62; *R.* v. *Knowlsey B.C., ex p. Maguire* [1992] 142 N.L.J. 1375 (Schiemann J.). See also, Harry Street, *Governmental Liability: a comparative study* (1953), pp. 78-80; Carol Harlow, *Compensation and Government Torts* (1982).

[9] Cases C-6/90 & 9/90, *Francovich* v. *Italian Republic* [1992] I.R.L.R. 84 (E.J.C.); *Kirklees M.B.C.* v. *Wickes Building Supplies Ltd.* [1992] 3 W.L.R. 170 (H.L.).

Arrangement of the Paper

1.6   Part A of this paper concerns the various problematical matters that have arisen regarding the procedure for judicial review. We comment on the background relevant to these matters, the problems and issues which they pose and where relevant, the options for reform on which we seek the views of consultees. The space devoted to different issues in the paper reflects the complexity of the law reform considerations rather than the intrinsic importance of the issue. Certain key issues, such as that of public policy, the European dimension and the fear of ever increasing case load, are recurrent factors and so are outlined at the outset in our introductory section. Following the sections relating to individual problematic issues, we provide a summary.

1.7   The second part of our review (Part B) considers whether there is scope for rationalising the great array of statutory provisions which give access to the High Court on appeal or by case stated or by application from the decision of an inferior court, tribunal or other body. We are primarily concerned with the principle of rationalisation and are interested in the purposes served by the different procedures and their effectiveness in enabling appeals and applications to be brought before the High Court. We feel that there are lessons to be learned from considering what may loosely be described as statutory rights of appeal alongside judicial review. If there is support for the principle of rationalisation, we seek consultees' views as to how to take the matter forward. We also comment briefly in Part B on the present scope of Crown Office proceedings.

PART A

JUDICIAL REVIEW

2   **INTRODUCTION**

Public Policy

2.1   The discussion of individual aspects of the supervisory jurisdiction by way of judicial review which follows (most particularly in relation to procedural exclusivity,[1] time limits[2] and interim relief[3]) shows that policy is a continual theme in the public law sphere. Judicial review often involves values and policy interests, which must be balanced against and may transcend the individual interests, which are normally the subject of litigation between private citizens. It is also a feature of the supervisory jurisdiction that its remedies are discretionary.[4]

2.2   Rules about judicial review procedure and its remedies are influenced by considerations of the balance between the interests of the individuals affected by a decision and public interests. The effectiveness or otherwise of the procedure is largely affected by one's view as to whether the courts' supervisory control achieves a *proper* balance between these interests. To this extent the parts of the law that we review, although in one sense procedural, have an important bearing on the limitations on the substantive relief provided by judicial review.

2.3   The competing public policy interests include:

(a)   the importance of vindicating the rule of law, so that public law bodies take lawful decisions and are prevented from relying on invalid decisions;

(b)   the need for speed and certainty in administrative decision-making in cases where the whole community, or large sections of it, will be affected by the decisions of public law bodies;

(c)   the private interest of individual litigants in obtaining a remedy for their grievances.

---

[1]   See section 3.

[2]   See section 4.

[3]   See section 6.

[4]   See section 14.

There might also be said to be a public interest in the prompt adjudication of disputes through the courts.

2.4   The balance between these interests is reflected by the specific requirements of the Order 53 procedure and the approach of the court to the exercise of its discretion to grant or refuse a public law remedy. It may also be affected by the nature and context of a case. Thus, the factor of certainty will be more important (although not necessarily decisive) where the act that is challenged is a general one, such as an administrative rule or a decision affecting a wide range of persons who may have relied on it.

2.5   The public interest in the vindication of the rule of law underpins the very existence of the prerogative jurisdiction and its supervisory role over inferior courts and decision-makers. The conferral of decision-making powers on lower courts and tribunals is to a certain extent premised upon the residual jurisdiction of the High Court to supervise and correct errors.

2.6   Many of the problematic issues concerning the present procedure reflect the tensions between differing interests. Lord Diplock, in *O'Reilly* v. *Mackman*,[5] commented that, both before and after the 1977 reforms, the procedure for judicial review provided respondent decision-making bodies with protection against claims which it was not in the public interest for courts of justice to entertain.

> "The public interest in good administration requires that public authorities and third parties should not be kept in suspense as to the legal validity of a decision the authority has reached in purported exercise of decision-making powers for any longer period than is absolutely necessary in fairness to the person affected by the decision."[6]

2.7   The public interest in good administration is concerned with the regular flow of consistent decisions, made and published with reasonable dispatch; in citizens knowing where they stand, and how they can order their affairs in the light of relevant decisions. In *R.* v. *Dairy Produce Tribunal, ex p. Caswell*,[7] Lloyd L.J. stated (in the context of the statutory provision on delay) that for there to be detriment to good administration:[8] "mere inconvenience is not enough. The foreseen consequence must be positive harm".[9] That detriment is a factor does not provide protection against mere inconvenience to the decision-maker or the

---

[5]   [1983] 2 A.C. 237, considered in section 3 below.

[6]   *Ibid.*, at 280H-281A.

[7]   [1990] 2 A.C. 738, considered in section 4 below.

[8]   Supreme Court Act 1981, section 31(6).

[9]   [1989] 1 W.L.R. 1089, 1100 (C.A.).

decision-making process. It is relevant to look at the wider scene, the impact on others, and the practicability of reopening a decision after a lapse of time.[10] This approach is also relevant to other aspects of the supervisory jurisdiction, in particular the exercise of discretion to grant or refuse a public law remedy.[11]

2.8   Sections 3 to 14 below consider the operation of these policy factors in the context of particular aspects of the judicial review procedure. The way these factors are balanced is also affected by the nature and context of a case. Given the importance of public policy in the exercise of the prerogative jurisdiction, consultees may wish to comment on the degree to which they consider that the procedures in general or in any particular respect reflect a proper balance between the competing interests inherent in the public sphere.

The European dimension in administrative law reform

2.9   There is an ever increasing awareness of the need to consider the principles relevant in EC law in any law reform exercise concerning administrative law. By virtue of the European Communities Act 1972, directly effective provisions of EC law which give rise to individual rights can be relied on in legal proceedings in the United Kingdom,[12] and questions as to the validity or meaning of a Community provision have to be determined according to EC law principles.[13] National law must not make it impossible or excessively difficult to enforce such rights.[14] Thus, in the provisions of R.S.C., Order 53 and section 31 of the Supreme Court Act 1981, which embody procedures governing access to remedies of substantial significance, EC law principles have to be taken into account in cases involving rights conferred by EC law.

2.10   It is also necessary to consider whether differences between domestic English law and EC law give rise to difficulties such as those concerning interim relief which arose in *R.* v. *Secretary of State for Transport, ex parte Factortame Ltd (No. 2)* (hereinafter refered to as *Factortame (No. 2)*).[15] Although it can be argued that

---

[10]   *R.* v. *Dairy Produce Tribunal, ex p. Caswell* [1990] 2 A.C. 738, 749-750 (Lord Goff).

[11]   See section 14 below.

[12]   Section 2(1).

[13]   Section 3(1).

[14]   Case 199/82, *Amministrazione delle Finanze dello Stato* v. *SpA San Giorgio* [1983] E.C.R. 3595; Case 309/85, *Barra* v. *Belgium* [1988] 2 C.M.L.R. 409.

[15]   [1991] 1 A.C. 603, discussed at paras. 6.4 - 6.6 below.

there is nothing wrong in principle with having different rules in cases which involve a question of European law, since *Factortame (No. 2)* senior judges have pointed to divergence from EC law as a justification for changing domestic law.[16] On this approach, our membership of the Community gives EC law a greater role as an indicator of possible avenues of reform than other systems of law which might be considered in a comparative manner. We invite views as to whether this is the correct premise to be adopted in considering EC law in a law reform exercise or whether, in the context of judicial review procedure, differences between domestic law and EC law are justifiable, and, if so, why.

2.11   The European Convention on Human Rights is not enforceable in legal proceedings in the United Kingdom.[17] However, similar considerations to those concerning EC law arise in connection with the entitlement that civil rights be determined in a fair and public hearing before an independent tribunal within a reasonable time[18] and to an effective remedy before a national authority in respect of rights under the Convention.[19]

Advisory Declarations

2.12   The need for citizens and authorities to 'know where they stand', identified above as being part of the public interest in good administration, may be relevant to the courts' jurisdiction to adjudicate on matters where the exercise of statutory or prerogative power is not being directly challenged. In private law it has been held that the courts' interest in the matter before it is exhausted by the private dispute at issue.[20] In public law, however, there may be circumstances in which the court will exercise a discretion to adjudicate even if circumstances have made the issue

---

[16]   *M* v. *Home Office* [1992] Q.B. 270, 360G-307A (Lord Donaldson M.R.); *Woolwich Equitable Building Society* v. *I.R.C.* [1992] 3 W.L.R. 366, 395-396 (Lord Goff).

[17]   But both statute law and common law will be interpreted, so far as possible, with a predilection that such law should conform with the principles of the Convention: *Derbyshire County Council* v. *Times Newspapers Ltd.* [1992] Q.B. 770 (now under appeal to the House of Lords).

[18]   Article 6(1).

[19]   Article 13. See generally, P.van Dijk and G.J.H.van Hoof, *Theory and Practice of the European Convention on Human Rights* (2nd ed., 1990), pp. 294 ff., and 520 ff..

[20]   *Sun Life Assurance Co. of Canada* v. *Jervis* [1944] A.C. 111.

to some extent academic.[21] The courts have also been willing to review advice guidance, for instance government circulars which in themselves have no direct legal effect.[22] The case of *R.* v. *Secretary of State for the Environment, ex p. Greenwich London Borough Council*,[23] which concerned a government community charge information leaflet, suggests that the courts' jurisdiction to review documents of this kind may extend beyond an examination of the legality of the action that they recommend to a review of the legality of their contents. However, it has been held that the court has no jurisdiction to grant a declaration amounting to an advisory opinion, for instance as to the scope of a public body's powers, even though a clear issue of law arose.[24]

2.13   In the light of these judicial developments, we invite consultees' views on what scope there should be for the courts to grant a declaration where there is no decision to be impugned. The power to grant 'advisory opinions' may be of considerable aid to public authorities and individuals faced with the interpretation of complex statutes drafted in very general terms (particularly those stemming from EC law), but would also have to take account of the long-standing tradition that the courts do not enter into purely hypothetical questions.[25]

The pressure of case-load on law reform options

2.14   As well as issues of principle, developed both domestically and in EC terms, we are also aware of the very practical pressures which influence the court's regulation of procedural law. In 1980 there were 525 applications for leave to move for judicial review, in 1984 there were 918, and in 1991 there were 2089 such applications.[26] This trend was maintained in 1992: in the first ten months there were 2034 applications for leave, compared with 1708 for the same period in 1991.[27] In 1992 there were, at any one time, on average two Divisional Courts

---

21   *R.* v. *Board of Visitors of Dartmoor Prison, ex p. Smith* [1987] Q.B. 106. But cf. para. 7.4 below for a contrasting situation in the context of mental health.

22   See *Royal College of Nursing* v. *D.H.S.S.* [1981] A.C. 800 and *Gillick* v. *West Norfolk and Wisbeach Area Health Authority* [1986] A.C. 112.

23   [1989] C.O.D. 530.

24   *R.* v. *Secretary of State for Education and Science, ex p. Birmingham C.C.* (14 May 1991, Brooke J.); *R.* v. *Secretary of State for Defence, ex p. Equal Opportunities Commission* [1992] C.O.D. 276 (Div. Ct.).

25   *Re Bernato* [1949] Ch. 259, 270 (*per* Lord Greene).

26   Before *O'Reilly* v. *Mackman* [1983] 2 A.C. 237, a number of public law cases would have been brought by writ or originating summons, but it is not possible to determine how many from the judicial statistics. On the case-load between 1981-1986, see M.Sunkin, "What is Happening to Applications for Judicial Review?", (1987) 50 M.L.R. 432.

27   We are grateful to the Crown Office for the figures for 1992.

and two (occasionally three) judges dealing with Crown Office business, i.e. with statutory appeals as well as judicial review.[28]

2.15 There have been calls from the judiciary[29] to devise procedural reform with the explicit purpose of reducing the burden of the case load. However, reform of the procedure for judicial review can only address case load problems to a limited extent. For example, many unarguable judicial review applications are initiated because there is no other mechanism of legal challenge open to the applicant. They are in substance disguised appeals. Cases on homelessness are often cited as an example. The proposed removal of certain rights of appeal in the Asylum and Immigration Appeals Bill 1992[30] is, if enacted, likely to lead to an increased number of applications for judicial review. This paper is not, however, concerned with whether Parliament should provide some form of appeal to a court or tribunal, although we invite views as to whether it is, in principle, desirable to make such provision.

2.16 On the other hand, there are certain aspects of the judicial allocation of the existing case load which might be amenable to improvement. We believe that it would be wrong to narrow the rules governing the availability of judicial review solely to meet problems of delay. Given the continuing increase in the case load and the perceived need to prevent the frustration of administrative action by delays[31] which are now approaching two years in cases for which expedition is not ordered, there are four ways in which it might be possible to reduce such delays.

2.17 The first is that arrangements might be made whereby the specially assigned or "nominated" judges regularly sit a minimum of a given number of weeks each year as single judges in the Crown Office List, following the practice adopted by the judges assigned to the Commercial Court. We are told for example, that because of the demands of other duties in the Queen's Bench Division, two of the 18 nominated judges in 1991 sat for a total of 3 weeks between them as single judges handling Crown Office cases, and others would not have sat very much more often.

2.18 The second is that more judges in the Queen's Bench Division might be nominated to do this work, or that judges in the Family Division or the Chancery Division might assist with this work.

---

28   The figures for other Crown Office business to the end of September 1992 (1991 figures in brackets) are: cases stated 132 (142), planning and other statutory appeals and applications 353 (365). The annual totals for 1991 were: cases stated 199, planning and other statutory appeals and applications 580.

29   See, in particular, Sir Harry Woolf, "Judicial Review: A Possible Programme for Reform", [1992] P.L. 221. See also *R.* v. *Panel on Takeovers and Mergers, ex p. Guinness plc* [1990] 1 Q.B. 146, 177-8 (Lord Donaldson M.R.).

30   Clauses 9-10.

31   Hansard, (H.L.), 22 October 1992, vol. 539, cols. 875 (Lord Irvine of Lairg Q.C.), 878 (Lord Taylor of Gosforth C.J.) and 883 (Lord Donaldson of Lymington).

2.19   The third, as Lord Woolf has suggested, is that certain types of judicial review applications would be more appropriately dealt with locally, rather than in London. and could be properly heard by judges other than the nominated judges.

2.20   The fourth, is that certain types of judicial review applications could properly be dealt with by selected circuit judges and Queens Counsel who have experience in the type of work in question, sitting as deputy high court judges. Queens Counsel experienced in planning law have been hearing statutory appeals in planning cases for some time now, and in the last four months of 1992 those experienced in administrative law have been assigned as an experiment to hear certain homelessness cases arising under the Housing Act. In each case there has been a substantial reduction in the backlog of cases awaiting disposal, although the arrangements have the disadvantage that High Court judges will seldom, if ever, be assigned to such cases because of the much greater delay that will be involved.

2.21   There are two issues:

(a)   the degree of centralisation necessary for the effective handling of the prerogative jurisdiction, and

(b)   the extent to which case-load difficulties could be addressed by arrangements whereby nominated judges sat more regularly to hear cases in the Crown Office list; or, without losing the expertise gained from the system of nominated judges, by looking more frequently beyond their number of the High Court judiciary as a whole or to selected circuit judges and Queens Counsel sitting as deputy High Court judges.

2.22   We invite views as to whether it would be acceptable in principle to facilitate the making of judicial review applications to High Court judges when on circuit outside London, to broaden the capacity of the High Court judge power available in London to hear such cases by arrangements whereby all the nominated judges sit hearing cases in the Crown Office List more frequently each year, or whereby other judges, in all three Divisions, are appointed to assist in this work, or to look beyond the nominated judges and the High Court judiciary as a whole to selected deputy high court judges in certain categories of case.

2.23   Another way of addressing the case load would be by delegating judicial review jurisdiction in certain prescribed cases to a lower court. This would, however, be contrary to the approach taken by the Civil Justice Review[32] which, in 1988, recommended that public law cases should continue to be heard only in the High Court.

---

[32]   Report of the Review Body on Civil Justice (1988), Cm. 394, paras. 120, 124.

3.1   Perhaps the most significant issue arising in relation to the procedures relevant to judicial review is the effect of the decision in *O'Reilly* v. *Mackman*.[1] In general terms this established that an applicant seeking one of the remedies provided by R.S.C., Order 53 must do so within the procedural constraints of that Order. The addition of declarations and injunctions to the remedies available to the court hearing applications for the prerogative remedies introduced an overlap between the power to seek declarations and injunctions in ordinary civil proceedings, and under the judicial review procedure. *O'Reilly* established the general rule that claims for declarations or injunctions relating essentially to public law matters must be brought under Order 53. To this extent *O'Reilly* made Order 53 an exclusive procedure. When we refer below to the 'principle of procedural exclusivity' we are referring to the general rule established in *O'Reilly* and not to a more comprehensive rule that would seek to divide all non-criminal causes and actions into two categories: 'essentially private law' and 'essentially public law', *each* with its own exclusive procedure.

3.2   Rights ordinarily classified as private law rights include proprietary, contractual, restitutionary and tortious rights. Rights to a non-discretionary remedy under statute, for example an action for damages for breach of statutory duty or for recompense for the performance of statutorily prescribed functions, are also regarded as private rights. There is, however, considerable uncertainty as to when a statute will, in the absence of express words, be held to create such a right as opposed to a "public law" right, the vindication of which is subject to the court's discretion and the policy considerations mentioned in section 2 above. As will be shown, there are, moreover, situations in which the two sorts of rights are closely interrelated. Until the decision in *O'Reilly* it was not necessary to make a distinction between public law and private law rights for procedural purposes and it was not common to characterise rights in these terms.[2]

3.3   The main issue for law reform consideration is the justification for the principle of procedural exclusivity and whether it ought to be retained. This we address by reference to the following:

(a)   the need which public authorities charged with the carrying out of statutory tasks have for special protection against litigation which prevents them from exercising their statutory tasks;

(b)   whether the exclusivity rule best addresses that need;

---

[1]   [1983] 2 A.C. 237.

[2]   *Davy* v. *Spelthorne B.C.* [1984] A.C. 262, 276 (per Lord Wilberforce).

(c)   the proper scope of exclusivity;

(d)   the dividing line between exclusivity and the assertion of public law issues (whether as a defence or otherwise) which arise collaterally in other proceedings;

We also consider in paragraphs 3.13 - 3.15 below whether challenges to public bodies acting in a private law capacity should be excluded from Order 53.

Background

3.4   The Commission's 1976 review of this topic stated a preference for devising a new procedure based on the existing procedure for prerogative orders which was relatively simple, inexpensive and speedy in comparison with writ proceedings.[3] The Commission was persuaded that the new procedure should not be exclusive in the sense of becoming the only way by which issues relating to the acts or omissions of public authorities could come before the courts.[4] However, the requirement of leave and the time limit present under Order 53 but absent in proceedings by writ or originating summons express divergent policy judgments as to the conditions under which a remedy may be obtained in public law. One commentator stated that,

> "The Law Commission ... failed fully to reason through the implications of their own reforms. ...[The] courts were placed in a dilemma. On the one hand, they could treat the procedure as non-exclusive. The consequences would however be odd. Precisely the same factual situations would be treated in radically different ways depending on which remedial route the applicant chose." [5]

It was perhaps inevitable that attempts would be made to prevent the requirements of the prerogative procedure from being circumvented.

3.5   In *O'Reilly*, four prisoners brought civil proceedings claiming declarations that the decision of a prison Board of Visitors on forfeiture of remission breached the rules of natural justice. The respondents contended that the civil proceedings were an abuse of process and that the only remedy was by judicial review which was subject to the constraints of Order 53. The House of Lords held that as a general rule it would be contrary to public policy and an abuse of process to pursue claims of infringement of public law rights by civil proceedings; in such cases judicial

---

[3]   Report on Remedies in Administrative Law (1976), Law Com. No.73.

[4]   *Ibid.*, para. 34.

[5]   P.P. Craig, *Administrative Law* (2nd ed., 1989), p. 425.

review should be the exclusive procedure.[6] The applicants had no private law rights; they were asserting a legitimate expectation which gave them a sufficient interest in public law to challenge the legality of the adverse decision as to remission.

3.6   The 1977 reforms had, in Lord Diplock's judgment, remedied the procedural disadvantages relating to discovery and cross-examination which had hitherto justified the courts permitting the continuation of an overlap in the manner in which such challenges should be raised, and led the House of Lords to reassert the need for protection of public authorities in the manner provided by the new judicial review procedure. The justification for such protection was

> "...the need, in the interests of good administration and of third parties who may be indirectly affected by the decision, for speedy certainty as to whether it has the effect of a decision that is valid in public law".[7]

Lord Diplock recognised that there would be exceptions to the rule, either where invalidity is raised collaterally in proceedings where private law rights are being asserted, or where no objection is taken, or in other situations that would be developed on a case by case basis.

3.7   *Cocks* v. *Thanet D.C.*,[8] a case concerning the duties of housing authorities to homeless persons, which was decided at the same time as *O'Reilly*, suggested that the exclusivity rule would apply to many situations raising a combination of public law and private law issues. However, it has since been regarded as a case in which purely public law issues were being contested. Sir John Donaldson M.R. analysed the decision as turning on the fact that the plaintiff's private law right in consequence of the statutory duty to house him only arose if two things happened: first that the court determined the public law issue in his favour and second that the authority made a further administrative decision favourable to him. When asserting his challenge in litigation, the plaintiff was not in a position to allege a private law right, only a public law one.[9] There have also been a number of complex cases in which *Cocks* has been distinguished in various ways.[10]

---

6   [1983] 2 A.C. 237, 285D-E (*per* Lord Diplock).

7   [1983] 2 A.C. 237, 284F.

8   [1983] 2 A.C. 286.

9   *An Bord Bainne Co-operative Limited* v. *Milk Marketing Board* [1984] 2 C.M.L.R. 584, 588.

10   *Davy* v. *Spelthorne B.C.* [1984] A.C. 262; *Wandsworth L.B.C.* v. *Winder* [1985] A.C. 461; *Roy* v. *Kensington and Chelsea and Westminster F.P.C.* [1992] 1 A.C. 624, 628-9 (*per* Lord Bridge). But cf., in the context of homelessness, *Ali* v. *Tower Hamlets L.B.C.* [1992] 3 All E.R. 512 and *Tower Hamlets L.B.C.* v. *Abdi, The Times*, 26 October 1992.

3.8   The most difficult analyses relate to those cases raising a combination of public law and private law issues. These difficulties are not helped by the fact that courts do not always identify to what extent their decisions are justified by reference to the true nature of the claim or to the collateral nature of the public law issue.[11] There is as yet no clear collateral challenge exception being applied to the *O'Reilly* exclusivity principle. Instead, the courts have tended to uphold individuals' rights to private law proceedings where their private law rights have been altered but not created by a public law decision, and where the challenge to that decision is by way of defence not attack.[12]

3.9   In *Gillick* v. *West Norfolk A.H.A.*,[13] which concerned parental rights, there was disagreement as to the nature of the claim. Lord Scarman and Lord Fraser considered the public law element to be collateral in the sense of being a subsidiary part of an essentially private law claim. Accordingly, it fell explicitly within the exceptions to the exclusivity principle stated by Lord Diplock in *O'Reilly*. Lord Bridge and probably Lord Templeman considered that the plaintiff had no private law right but thought that the technicality as to the procedure could be disregarded, perhaps because the writ had been issued before the decision in *O'Reilly* and no procedural objection had been taken. Lord Brandon expressed no view.

3.10   In *Wandsworth L.B.C.* v. *Winder*[14], on the other hand, the House of Lords held that the invalidity of an administrative decision increasing the rent payable by the council's tenants formed the whole basis of the defence, and could not properly be regarded as subsidiary. Nevertheless, the applicant's private law proceedings were not struck out as an abuse of process because, it was said, he was merely seeking to defend proceedings brought against him.[15] The House of Lords' reasoning in *Winder* has been criticised by Lord Woolf: if a public law issue can be raised simply as a defence in other non-Crown proceedings, rather than as an independent

---

11   *Davy* v. *Spelthorne B.C.* [1984] A.C. 262; *Doyle* v. *Northumbria Probation Committee* [1991] 1 W.L.R. 1340; *Woolwich Equitable Building Society* v. *I.R.C.* [1992] 3 W.L.R. 366 (discussed at para. 10.2 below).

12   Cf. *Cocks* v. *Thanet D.C* [1983] 2 A.C. 286..

13   [1986] A.C. 112.

14   [1985] A.C. 461, 508B, *per* Lord Fraser.

15   See also *D.P.P.* v. *Hutchinson* [1990] 2 A.C. 783 (which decided that the invalidity of parts of certain legislative instruments could not be cured by severance and could be raised as a defence in criminal proceedings). For an earlier and different approach, see *Quietlynn Ltd.* v. *Plymouth C.C.* [1988] Q.B. 114. Cf. *R.* v. *Reading Crown Court, ex p. Hutchinson* [1988] Q.B. 384 and in the context of homelessness *Tower Hamlets L.B.C.* v *Abdi, The Times*, 26 October 1992.

issue its own right, it will not be fully examined in the way in which it would have been within the framework and safeguards of judicial review.[16] The criticism appears to be based on the view that the tenant in *Winder* had no private law right because his right to pay only the rent specified in his tenancy agreement had been removed by the local authority's decision increasing the rent. This, however, involves treating an ultra vires decision affecting private rights as effective unless and until the court intervenes in judicial review proceedings.

3.11   *Roy* v. *Kensington and Chelsea and Westminster F.P.C.*[17] also explores the scope of the *O'Reilly* exclusivity rule. This case concerned the entitlement of a doctor to remuneration, the basic practice allowance, prescribed by statutory instrument. Lord Lowry discussed two possible interpretations of the exclusivity rule. The "broad approach" was that Order 53 would only be insisted upon if private rights were not in issue; the "narrow approach" on the other hand requiring applicants to proceed by judicial review in all proceedings in which public law acts or decisions were challenged (even collaterally) subject to some exceptions where private law rights were involved.[18]   Lord Bridge was of the view that the incidental involvement of a public law issue in private law claims could not debar the plaintiff from taking civil proceedings.[19]

3.12   The House of Lords did not decide which approach was the correct one. Lord Lowry's conclusion that unless the procedure is ill suited to the disposal of the issue, the court should let the case proceed and not debate the form of the proceedings, may herald a change from the formal characterisation of claims in favour of a more pragmatic approach to the policy issues raised in *O'Reilly v. Mackman*.[20] It might, however, also be fair to suggest that the difficulties arising from the decision in *O'Reilly* have arisen in part from the limited consideration given by the House of Lords to the procedural implications of an exclusivity rule. The Court of Appeal has recently held that there was no need to apply for judicial review before asserting a private law right arising out of a background of public

---

16   "Public Law - Private Law: Why the Divide? A Personal View", [1986] P.L. 220, 234-235. Cf para. 3.9 above.

17   [1992] 1 A.C. 624, noted by S.Fredman and G.Morris, "A Snake or a Ladder? *O'Reilly* v. *Mackman* Reconsidered", (1992) 108 L.Q.R. 353.

18   [1992] 1 A.C. 624, 653.

19   *Ibid.*, 628H-9A.

20   *Ibid.*, 654D and 655A. The ingenuity of courts in overriding procedural issues in order to overcome the particular problem faced in a case was commented on by Lord Woolf in "Judicial Review: A Possible Programme for Reform", [1992] P.L. 221, p. 231, citing *Chief Adjudication Officer* v. *Foster* [1992] 1 Q.B. 31 and *R.* v. *Secretary of State for the Home Department, ex p. Muboyayi* [1992] Q.B. 244.

15

law. The decision in *Roy's* case was welcomed since the law was said to have "suffered too much from the undesirable complexities of [an] over legalistic procedural dichotomy".[21]

3.13   In all the above cases the essential question was the scope of the general rule laid down in *O'Reilly* - *Roy* may be said to be a pragmatic compromise between the policy of restricting public authorities' exposure to public law challenge and the protection of private law rights. However in addition to pursuing this policy of forcing a certain class of challenges into the Order 53 procedure courts have also *excluded* another class of challenges - those deemed to be 'essentially private law' matters - from the procedure for judicial review, even where both the applicant and the respondent wish to proceed by judicial review.[22] In *R.* v. *East Berkshire H.A., ex parte Walsh*[23] the court applied what was termed by the Master of the Rolls the 'obverse' of the rule in *O'Reilly* v. *Mackman.*[24] Judicial review was declared to be an inappropriate means of challenging a public authority when that authority is acting in the capacity of a private contracting party. The applicant sought certiorari to quash a health authority's decision to dismiss him, claiming that the district nursing officer had no power to dismiss him and that there had been breaches of natural justice in the dismissal procedure. Perhaps with the ruling in *O'Reilly* in mind, Walsh exposed himself to all the procedural restrictions designed to protect the public authority he was challenging, only to find his case categorised as essentially one of private law and therefore a misuse of the Order 53 procedure. The Court of Appeal also declined to exercise their discretion to transfer the applicant into writ proceedings via rule 9(5), the 'anti-technicality rule', because he had sought only certiorari and not a declaration.

3.14   The problem raised by this case is that applicants in Walsh's position cannot know at the outset whether the challenged public body will raise issues of public law in answer to their statement of claim or not. If Walsh had begun writ proceedings, with its attendant procedural advantages, seeking a declaration that the authority had acted ultra vires in delegating the power to dismiss to a district nursing officer, the authority might easily have responded that this delegation, or indeed other matters leading up to the dismissal, were matters of public law which could only be questioned in judicial review proceedings.

---

[21]   *Lonrho Plc.* v. *Tebbit* [1992] 4 All E.R. 280, 288 (Sir Michael Kerr).

[22]   *R.* v. *Durham C.C., ex p. Robinson, The Times,* 31 January 1992.

[23]   [1985] Q.B. 152. See also *R.* v. *Secretary of State for the Home Department, ex p. Benwell* [1985] Q.B. 554 and *R.* v. *British Broadcasting Corporation, ex p. Lavelle* [1983] 1 W.L.R. 23.

[24]   [1985] Q.B. 152, 159G.

16

3.15   The prerogative writs were not previously available to enforce private rights[25] but injunction and declaration could lie against domestic tribunals.[26] The main justification for excluding claims against bodies acting under private law obligations from the ambit of the modern judicial review procedure would be one based on the appropriate allocation of judicial resources. However if the courts choose to follow the "narrow approach" to the *O'Reilly* rule - requiring applicants to proceed by judicial review in all cases in which public law acts or decisions are challenged (even collaterally) - as described by Lord Lowry in *Roy,* then it appears somewhat harsh to label as "abuses of the court" those cases which subsequently resolve themselves into predominantly private law disputes. One answer to this problem might be a more flexible switching procedure which we discuss below (see paragraphs 3.24 - 3.26).

Issues

3.16   We have commented on the different public policy interests which have influenced the development of the procedure for judicial review.[27] Different attitudes to the relative need to vindicate the rule of law, or for speed and certainty for the benefit of the wider community, or for the protection of the personal interest of the litigant are particularly influential in the views which have been adopted as to the proper scope of the exclusivity principle. *O'Reilly* gave high priority to the need for speedy certainty in administrative decision-making. In *Roy,* the different emphasis given to the private rights of an individual tended to suggest that the exclusivity principle was more limited and was subject to a wider category of exceptions.

3.17   Three criticisms have been made of the principle of exclusivity:

(a)   Any exclusivity rule operates by automatically protecting public authorities, without reference to the actual degree of administrative inconvenience liable to be suffered.

(b)   The existence of an exclusivity rule suggests that a sharp distinction can be drawn between private law rights and public law rights which can or cannot be raised in civil litigation. This is not true, and is liable to generate

---

[25]   *R.* v. *British Broadcasting Corporation, ex p. Lavelle* [1983] 1 W.L.R. 23, 30 *per* Woolf J..

[26]   *Lee* v. *The Showmen's Guild of Great Britain* [1952] 2 Q.B. 329, 346.

[27]   See section 2.

17

needless litigation over procedural issues, rather than the substance of the dispute.[28]

(c) The exclusivity rule has been justified on the ground that the protection afforded to public authorities by the requirement of leave and short time limits is required to protect public authorities against litigation which prevents them from carrying out their statutory tasks. Although this justification might be thought to be equally applicable to litigation in which the infringement of rights in tort or contract is asserted, public authorities are not accorded special protection from such litigation.[29]

3.18 The problems which arise from the principle of procedural exclusivity are closely linked with those relevant to time limits and the requirement of leave. It is because of the more restrictive time limits and the conditional nature of the power to raise a challenge which were introduced by *O'Reilly* when the remedy of either a declaration or injunction in public law is sought, that the principle of exclusivity has caused such controversy.

Options for reform

3.19 There are different ways in which reform might be approached. It is necessary first to form a view as to whether the exclusivity principle is the correct principle to apply, i.e. whether *O'Reilly* is to be upheld or departed from. Thereafter the proper scope of the exclusivity principle has to be considered.

(a) The exclusivity principle might simply be abolished without any reformulation of the need for special handling of challenges of a public nature. This would expose public bodies to the same liability to declaratory and injunctive remedies as respondents in civil litigation.

(b) Alternatively, the principle could be extended to all proceedings for declarations and injunctions against public authorities.

(c) A third alternative would be to specify more clearly the boundaries of the application of the principle, perhaps in terms of the necessary compromise between the competing policy interests of legality and certainty.

---

[28] JUSTICE-All Souls Report, *op. cit.* p. 150, para. 6-20.

[29] e.g. *Hotson* v. *East Berkshire A.H.A.* [1987] A.C. 750. See generally, P.P. Craig, *Administrative Law* (2nd ed., 1989) pp. 422-423.

3.20   The application of the exclusivity principle has been considered by the House of Lords on six different occasions during the last ten years, and yet no clear picture of its scope has emerged. It is not surprising, therefore, that there are continuing doubts as to whether the principle of exclusivity is the correct one to protect the issues of public policy identified by the House of Lords in *O'Reilly*. If it is not, it may be that it should be departed from, avoiding further sterile procedural argument in the higher courts, and perhaps allowing a different and more fruitful principle to emerge.

3.21   If the exclusivity principle were to be dispensed with, and the special position of public authorities ceased to be protected as a matter of general policy (except where the particular circumstances justified such protection), it has been suggested that it would be possible to develop the procedure for striking out claims to provide the necessary safeguarding of the public interest.[30] Grounds for striking out might include excessive administrative inconvenience, or the actual degree of inconvenience likely to arise in the particular circumstances of the case.

3.22   As regards the alternative of seeking to provide a clearer formulation of the scope of the exclusivity principle, there are several factors identifiable from the case law which might be of assistance, including the points referred to by Lord Lowry in *Roy*.[31] In summary, the relevant factors might be:

(a)   Whether the existence of a private law right depends on the exercise of the public authority's discretion in the applicant's favour - if yes, the proceedings should be brought by way of judicial review;

(b)   Whether private law rights and issues of fact dominate the proceedings, despite the existence of a claim seeking enforcement of performance of a public law duty - if so, Order 53 procedure should not be insisted upon.

(c)   Whether there are other matters in issue which could not be joined in a claim under Order 53.

3.23   We have commented on the present trend in the courts' attitude to scope, and the options for reform. The present trend is towards limiting insistence on use of Order 53 to claims raising issues solely of public law. We provisionally support this development and the balance which it seeks to promote, but we recognise that

---

[30]   This suggestion has been raised in various forms and by different commentators including, e.g. H.W.R. Wade, "Procedure and Prerogative in Public Law", (1985) 101 L.Q.R. 180. See, further, para. 5.9 below.

[31]   [1992] 1 A.C. 624, 654.

it does not eliminate the uncertainty and the potential for continuing litigation over procedural issues.

Transfer into, or out of, Order 53

3.24   Reform of the requirement of procedural exclusivity is so closely linked with the issues relating to the provisions for time limits and leave that consideration may need to be given to devising a facility for transfer between civil (or criminal) proceedings and Crown side proceedings.[32] The aim would be to overcome the procedural difficulties which have arisen following *O'Reilly* by ensuring that both the public law challenge and other issues arising in a particular case are fully addressed within the most appropriate procedure.

3.25   Order 53, rule 9(5) empowers the court to order the transfer out of Order 53 in appropriate cases but there is no provision for transfer into the judicial review procedure. We consider that it would be useful for there to be a power to transfer a case which only raises a public law issue or in which the existence of a private law right depends on the exercise of a public authority's discretion in the applicant's favour into the Queen's Bench Divisional Court. There would be ancillary procedural points to consider in the case of transfer into Order 53, in particular whether any of the Order 53 safeguards such as the three month time limit would be waived.

3.26   Another, related, development would be to consider whether there should be power to join two forms of proceedings so that all the issues could be properly determined and the remedies provided in one court.

---

[32]   The suggestion was made in the Court of Appeal by Lord Denning M.R. in *O'Reilly* v. *Mackman* [1983] 2 A.C. 237, 258.

4 TIME LIMITS

Background

4.1 Before 1977, the only prerogative remedy in respect of which there was an established time limit was certiorari. The time limit was six months, and whilst courts had discretion to grant the remedy beyond that limit, they rarely did so. When the six month time limit for certiorari applied, applications might be refused despite being brought within that period although this was said to be rare,[1] and the court might put the onus on the respondent to prove that there had been undue delay if the case was initiated within six months.[2] The jurisdiction to grant injunctions and declarations in civil proceedings was not subject to a limitation period, though in determining whether to grant discretionary remedies such as injunctions, declarations, and (in prerogative proceedings) mandamus, delay could be fatal.

4.2 In 1976, the Commission recommended that the court should not refuse relief solely on the grounds of delay unless the granting of the relief would cause substantial prejudice or hardship to any person or would be detrimental to good administration. The court was in effect asked to evaluate the relevance of delay. An exception was made where another enactment fixed a time limit; in such circumstances the time limit was the decisive factor.

4.3 Time limits provide a practical part of the balancing of public and private interests in the pursuit of a remedy. By identifying the imperative of speed, they emphasise the conditional nature of the individual's claim to be acting in the public interest. Where there has been delay the courts are, in the exercise of their discretion, attempting to weigh not administrative convenience, but the impact of further litigation on the public in general and the practicability of turning back the clock. The context and nature of a particular decision are important.[3]

4.4 The present provisions embodying the provisions for time limits are to be found in R.S.C., Order 53, rule 4 and section 31(6) and (7) of the Supreme Court Act 1981 (see Annex 1). The insertion of reference to a three month period in Order

---

[1] *R. v. Herrod, ex p. Leeds* [1976] Q.B. 540, 547.

[2] *R. v. Herrod, ex p. Leeds City Council* [1978] A.C. 403.

[3] On specific statutory time limits in a particular context (planning), see Part B para. 2.4 below.

53, rule 4(1) was a later amendment. The Commission's original formulation re-emerged in section 31 of the Supreme Court Act 1981 but, given rule 4(1), the effect was much tougher on applicants.[4]

Issues

4.5   The first issue which may require reconsideration is whether the choice of three months is the correct time limit. The Commission's 1976 Report recorded that consultation had shown a considerable measure of criticism of the six month period for certiorari, some consultees suggesting three years, others up to six years, i.e. a reversion to limitation periods applicable in civil proceedings.[5] If a time limit is to be retained, we invite views as to the length of the period. The period chosen must take account of the practical realities of the time needed to evaluate the merits of initiating a challenge and to approach the other side to discover the scope for settlement without recourse to the court. The three month period has been criticised,[6] and it has been suggested that the need for speed it imposes may encourage rather than deter misconceived applications and deter settlement.[7]

4.6   It may be, however, that the problem lies not in the actual length of the period, but the arbitrariness and inflexibility of any fixed period. This factor weighed particularly with the Commission in its 1976 Report. A fixed period (even with the retained judicial discretion to extend if merited) may cause injustice: applications may be refused leave even where only marginally out of time and where there has been no unnecessary delay.

4.7   The difficulties in reconciling section 31(6)and (7) on the one hand and R.S.C., Order 53, rule 4 on the other, were discussed in *R. v. Dairy Produce Tribunal, ex p. Caswell*.[8] Some of these difficulties have been resolved judicially. The differences are identified in the Table below.

---

[4]   There was a proposal to repeal section 31(6) of the 1981 Act as part of the proposed clause 43 of the Administration of Justice Bill 1985 which had to be withdrawn, due to the controversy as to another element in that clause concerning limitation of rights of appeal from refusal of leave to apply for judicial review.

[5]   Law Com. No. 73, para. 50.

[6]   JUSTICE-All Souls Report, *op. cit.*, pp. 155-157, paras. 6.28-6.31; P. Cane, *An Introduction to Administrative Law* (2nd ed.,1992), p. 91; P.P. Craig, *Administrative Law* (2nd ed.,1989), p. 423.

[7]   A.P. Le Sueur and M. Sunkin, "Applications for Judicial Review: The Requirement of Leave", [1992] P.L. 102, 105-106.

[8]   [1990] 2 A.C. 738, 746-747.

TABLE: COMPARISON OF THE TIME LIMIT PROVISIONS CONTAINED IN SECTION 31 OF THE SUPREME COURT ACT 1981 AND R.S.C., ORDER 53, RULE 4.

Matter referred to	Section 31(6) S.C.A. 1981	R.S.C., Order 53, rule 4
length of time limit	not referred to	three months for all judicial review applications + requirement of promptness
when time begins to run	not referred to	specified in relation to certiorari r.4(2)
reference to detriment to good administration and third party prejudice	yes	not referred to
reference to undue delay	yes	not referred to
distinguishes between the application for leave and the substantive application	applies to both stages	rule 4(1) applies only at the leave stage (see para. 4.8 below)
addressing the reasons justifying extension of the time limit	refers to the effects of delay as grounds for refusing relief	looks to the existence of good reason for extending the time limit
effect of other statutory time limits	section 31(7) is stated to be without prejudice to any enactment or rule of court having the effect of providing a time limit	rule 4(3) states that the rule is without prejudice to any statutory provision which has the effect of providing a time limit.

4.8   A distinction has been drawn between the hearing of an application for leave and the hearing of the substantive application. The phrase "an application for judicial review" in Order 53 is to be interpreted as meaning the application for leave.[9]

4.9   When an application for leave is not made promptly and in any event within three months, there has been undue delay for the purposes of section 31(6), and the court

---

[9]   R. v. *Stratford-on-Avon D.C., ex p. Jackson* [1985] 1 W.L.R. 1319 (C.A.); R. v. *Dairy Produce Quota Tribunal, ex p. Caswell* [1990] 2 A.C. 738.

23

may refuse to grant leave unless it considers that there is good reason for extending the period.[10] Lord Goff, in *Caswell*, suggested that it may be better for courts to extend the period under rule 4(1), leaving the issues of hardship, prejudice or detriment under section 31(6) to be explored in depth on the hearing of the substantive application.[11]

4.10 Matters which are still problematical include the date from which the time limit runs, the question of promptness, what constitutes good reason for extending time and the circumstances in which the court will exercise its discretion.

4.11 *The date from which the time limit runs*.[12] Although in the case of certiorari there is a formula by which to determine the commencement of the period, there is much uncertainty as regards the time limit in relation to other remedies. The uncertainty affects both the general approach adopted for mandamus, prohibition, declarations and injunctions, and the particular approach used in rules under specific statutes. As regards the latter, in different statutes it might be the date on which the rule was made, or published, or when the applicant found out about it or should have known about it, or some other date. Furthermore, the commencement of the period might also be affected if the applicant had prior warning of the decision or rule complained of.[13]

4.12 *The question of promptness*. Case law stresses that promptness is the dominant consideration. An application for leave, even if made within three months, may still be said to have not been made promptly.[14] Despite the existence of good reason for the delay, the court may still refuse to grant leave or substantive relief. Furthermore, the grant of leave does not preclude the court from ruling at the substantive hearing that there had been undue delay even where the issue of promptness had been argued and rejected by the court at the leave stage.[15]

---

[10] As well as *ex p. Caswell, ibid.*, see *R.* v. *Commissioner for Local Administration, ex p. Croydon L.B.C.* [1989] 1 All E.R. 1033, 1046; *R.* v. *Dairy Produce Quota Tribunal, ex p. Hood* [1990] C.O.D. 184, *R.* v. *Secretary of State for Transport, ex p. Presvac Engineering Ltd.* (1992) 4 Admin. L.R. 121.

[11] [1990] 2 A.C. 738, 747E.

[12] See *R.* v. *Secretary of State for Transport, ex p. Presvac Engineering Ltd.* (1992) 4 Admin. L.R. 121 (C.A.).

[13] *Re Friends of the Earth* [1988] J.P.L. 93, 94.

[14] *R.* v. *Independent Television Commission, ex p. TV NI Ltd., The Times*, 30 December 1991 (C.A.).

[15] *R.* v. *Swale Borough Council, ex p. Royal Society for the Protection of Birds* [1990] C.O.D. 263; *R.* v. *General Commissioners of Income Tax for Tavistock* (1985) 59 T.C. 116.

4.13 *What constitutes "good reason" for extending the time limit.* It has been said that "good reason" does not equate with "good excuse", and that leave may be refused on grounds of delay even where it is perfectly explicable. Good reason may justify extension of the time limit where, for example, the delay arose from pursuing an alternative remedy,[16] the need to obtain legal aid before commencing proceedings,[17] and correspondence with the Crown Court about another possible remedy.[18] The type of error may also be relevant.[19]

4.14 *The nature of the court's discretion under section 31(6).* As stated above, the court may refuse to grant leave, or the relief sought, if it considers that the granting of relief would be likely to cause substantial hardship to, or substantially prejudice the rights, of any person or would be detrimental to good administration in the sense of positive harm rather than mere inconvenience.[20] As regards the factors of hardship and prejudice, some cases have emphasised the prejudice to the rights of other persons,[21] whereas others have distinguished between distress and substantial prejudice, where the danger of challenge was known about at an early stage.[22] Apart from the length of time itself, matters of particular importance in considering whether relief should be granted despite the delay include the extent of the effect of the relevant decision and the impact which would be felt if it were to be re-opened.[23]

4.15 In *Caswell* the court reasoned that as the tribunal's decision related to the allocation of part of a finite amount of quota, the re-opening of that decision by the court would lead to the re-opening of the allocation of quota over a number of years, which after the elapse of time involved, would be detrimental to good

---

[16] *Ex p. Jackson* [1985] 1 W.L.R. 1319, see also *R.* v. *Rochdale Metropolitan Borough Council, ex p. Cromer Ring Mill Ltd.* [1982] 3 All E.R. 761. On alternative remedies, see section 14 below.

[17] *Ex p. Jackson, ibid..*

[18] *R.* v. *Lincoln Crown Court, ex p. Jones, The Times,* 16 June 1989.

[19] *R.* v. *Secretary of State for the Home Department, ex p. Ruddock* [1987] 1 W.L.R. 1482; *R.* v. *Minister of Agriculture, Fisheries and Food, ex p. Bostock* [1991] 1 C.M.L.R. 687.

[20] See para. 2.7 above.

[21] *R.* v. *Lewes Magistrates, ex p. Oldfield, The Times,* 6 May 1987.

[22] *R.* v. *Port Talbot Borough Council, ex p. Jones* [1988] 2 All E.R. 207.

[23] *R.* v. *Dairy Produce Tribunal, ex p. Caswell* [1989] 1 W.L.R. 1089, 1100.

administration.[24]   At first instance, Popplewell J. had outlined several (not exclusive) factors as relevant to the extension of time, including the length of delay, the excuse, the actions of the applicant (including his agent) and the respondent, further delay after initiating the application, the prejudice and hardship to the applicant, or to respondents and third parties of granting relief measured at the time when the court considers the issue, and the extent of detriment to good administration.

EC Law and other jurisdictions

4.16   Further light may be cast on the judicial understanding of the concept of good administration by comparison with the approach adopted in EC law to limiting the time within which administrative acts or rules laid down by EC institutions may be challenged. There is a central principle of legal certainty. The European Court of Justice has stated that

> "The limitation period for bringing an action fulfils a generally recognized need, namely the need to prevent the legality of administrative decisions from being called into question indefinitely, and this means that there is a prohibition on reopening a question after the limitation period has expired."[25]

4.17   It has also been suggested that such time limits meet the need to avoid any discrimination or arbitrary treatment in the administration of justice.[26] On the expiry of the time limit, usually between one and three months[27] from the publication or notification of the measure in question, a measure becomes formally valid, rendering it inadmissible to bring an action to challenge the validity of the measure.[28]

---

[24]   [1990] 2 A.C. 738, 750, *per* Lord Goff.

[25]   Case 3/59, *Federal Republic of Germany* v. *High Authority* [1960] E.C.R. 53,61. See also Case 156/67, *Commission* v. *Belgium* [1978] E.C.R. 1881, 1896.

[26]   Case 209/83, *Ferriera Valsabbia Case* [1984] E.C.R. 3089.

[27]   For a fuller account of the position relating to time limits, see H.G.Shermers and D.F. Waelbroeck, *Judicial Protection in the European Communities* (5th ed., 1992), pp. 54-56. Under Article 26 of the European Convention on Human Rights, the period is six months from the date of a final decision, on which see P van Dijk and G.J.H. van Hoof, *Theory and Practice of the European Convention on Human Rights*, (2nd ed., 1990), pp. 98 - 104.

[28]   For exceptions to the principle of formal validity see J.Schwarze, *European Administrative Law* (1992), p. 1044-1054.

4.18   In Scotland there is no special time limit. In Northern Ireland, R.S.C., (N.I.) Order 53, rule 4 states that where leave to apply has not been sought within three months, the court may not grant leave or relief unless it is satisfied that such a move would not cause hardship to or unfairly prejudice the rights of any person.[29]

4.19   In Canada, most jurisdictions do not impose a strict time limit, preferring to leave the question of delay to the court's discretion. In Nova Scotia and in Alberta, on the other hand, there is a strict six month time limit regarding an application for certiorari.[30] The court may refuse an application made within the six month period on the ground of undue delay, and the primary considerations here too are said to be the need for effective and reliable administration, and hardship and prejudice to third parties who have acted in good faith on the strength of an apparently valid decision.[31] The Law Reform Commission of Canada has recommended that periods for applying for and proceedings within judicial review should be fairly short but that the court should retain the power to extend the time.[32]

4.20   In New Zealand there is no express time limit, but the court has discretion to refuse relief if there has been undue delay. In Australia, the time limit varies: for the Commonwealth of Australia the period is generally 28 days, although the court has a wide discretion to extend it.[33] In New South Wales, there is no time limit. The Law Reform Commission of Western Australia has recommended a primary requirement that an applicant must commence proceedings promptly and in any event within six months, and that the six month period may be extended if there is good reason for doing so.[34]

4.21   In the United States, time limits are generally dealt with in the context of specific statutes rather than in administrative procedure Acts. At the Federal level, many

---

[29]   The Northern Ireland case law is analysed by B.Hadfield, "Delay in Applications for Judicial Review - A Northern Ireland Perspective", (1988) 7 C.J.Q. 189 and "Judicial Review in Northern Ireland: A Primer", (1991) 42 N.I.L.Q. 332.

[30]   Rule 56.06 of the Nova Scotia Civil Procedure Rules 1971 and Rule 742 of the Alberta Rules of Court.

[31]   D.P. Jones and A.S. de Villars, *Principles of Administrative Law* (1985) pp. 373-4; J.M.Evans, H.N. Janisch etc., *Administrative Law, Cases and Materials* (3rd ed., 1989), p.1075.

[32]   Report 14, *Judicial Review and the Federal Court* (1980), Recommendation 6.4.

[33]   Commonwealth Administrative Decisions (Judicial Review) Act 1977, s.11; D.C. Pearce, *Commonwealth Administrative Law* (1986), p.139, para. [355].

[34]   *Report on Judicial Review of Administrative Decisions: Procedural Aspects and the Right to Reasons* (1986), Project No. 26-Part II, ch.7, Recommendations 6-8.

statutes are modelled on the Federal Trade Commission Act 1914 which requires proceedings to be instituted within sixty days after the service of an order[35] although periods of thirty days are not uncommon.[36] As far as State law is concerned, it is commonly provided that petitions for judicial review of orders must be filed within thirty days, but, in the case of action other than orders or rules, that the period will be extended while the petitioner is exhausting administrative remedies.[37] The general review Statute in New York provides that all review actions must be instituted within four months.[37] In the case of administrative rules, the Model State Administrative Procedure Act 1981 provides no time limit on challenges to the substance of rules but a two year limit on challenges to their procedural adequacy.[38]

4.22   A question may be raised as to the time limits applicable where an applicant seeks to rely on directly enforceable EC rights in domestic courts. It is clear that national courts are required to protect rights arising from directly enforceable provisions of EC law.[39] It has been held that it is for the domestic legal system of each member state to determine the procedural conditions, including those relating to time limits where none has been laid down by Community law.[40] Time limits must be "reasonable" and should not be less favourable than those relating to similar actions involving purely domestic issues.[41] Where national authorities have failed to comply with a directly enforceable EC provision they are in any case prohibited from relying on any domestic time limit for the bringing of an action until their compliance is made good.[42] Similar considerations apply to rights under

---

[35]   15 U.S.C.A., para. 45. See generally, Schwartz, *Administrative Law*, (3rd ed., 1991) p. 472.

[36]   e.g. Federal Communications Commission Act 1934, 47 U.S.C.A., para. 402 and Clean Air Act 1970, 42 U.S.C.A., para. 7401.

[37]   W.R. Andersen, "Judicial Review of State Administrative Action - Designing the Statutory Framework", (1992) 44 Admin. L. Rev. 523, 539-40.

[37]   N.Y. Civ. Pr. L & R., para. 217.

[38]   Sections 3-113(b), 5-108.

[39]   Article 5 E.E.C. Treaty.

[40]   See Case 45/76, *Comet* [1976] E.C.R. 2043, 2053.

[41]   See Case 33/76, *Rewe* [1976] E.C.R. 1990, 1998. But it may be queried whether the presumption in favour of domestic legal certainty in *Rewe* and *Comet* is due to the fiscal context in which they arose.

[42]   See *Cannon* v. *Barnsley M.B.C.*, *The Times*, 24 June 1992, applying Case No. 208/90, *Emmott* v. *Minister for Social Welfare* [1991] 2 E.C. Cas. 395. In *R.* v. *Minister of Agriculture, Fisheries and Food, ex p. Bostock* [1991] 1 C.M.L.R. 687

the European Convention on Human Rights[43], although these are not directly enforceable in United Kingdom courts and the impact of such rights on procedure can only be indirect.

Options for reform

4.23   Our discussion of the position as regards EC law, as well as that in other jurisdictions identifies further factors relevant when considering the scope for reform. Emphasis on the principle of certainty and the protection of directly effective rights mirrors the competing desires for specified time limits and yet for flexibility.

4.24   The central issues would appear to us to be

(a)   whether three months is the correct period for judicial review applications;

(b)   whether the tests relating to delay currently applied are the most equitable that can be devised;

(c)   whether there should be a difference between the position of claims for injunctions and declarations in civil proceedings and that in proceedings for judicial review;

(d)   whether the balance between the time limit and the factor of delay is correctly drawn at present.

4.25   The JUSTICE-All Souls Report recommended that the time limit of three months should be removed and the focus should be placed entirely on the factor of delay.[44]

4.26   If a short maximum time limit is thought to be most appropriate, it might be cast with or without reference to the issue of delay. An example of the former is that which applies in Australia (one month) or for E.C. law. This is in effect the current law: a primary requirement of no delay, together with a subordinate requirement of bringing the claim in any event within three months.

---

leave was granted out of time where doubt had been cast on a decision by a subsequent EC instrument.

[43]   Articles 6(1) and 13.

[44]   *Op. cit.,* para. 6.30.

4.27   Whichever policy is favoured, consideration ought also to be given to ensuring that it is clearly formulated. Section 31 of the 1981 Act and Order 53, rule 4 have undoubtedly caused confusion and difficulties of interpretation. The position of those who do not institute judicial review proceedings because they are pursuing an alternative remedy could also be clarified.[45]

Provisional View

4.28   We do not consider that abandonment of time limits and reliance on limitation periods relevant in civil proceedings is a practical or desirable option. The principle of certainty is particularly important where the validity of regulations and the legality of decisions made by reviewable bodies is liable to be tested by litigation. Furthermore, the public policy considerations which require a balance to be struck between the rights of the individual, the vindication of the rule of law and the need for speed and administrative certainty all tend to justify the provision of special time limits for initiating legal challenges to administrative acts.

4.29   The case for giving effect to the principle of certainty by the provision of a specified time limit rests largely on pragmatic considerations. The period chosen must be a compromise between what will be regarded, by those having an interest in the implementation of decisions, as the necessary element of dispatch, and the different perspectives which applicants, respondents and third parties may have on the point.

4.30   Whilst the three month limit may be criticised as too short,[46] even shorter periods apply in relation to certain acts of EC institutions and in some other jurisdictions and the six week period applicable to statutory applications to quash is long established. We think that the correct balance lies somewhere between three to six months. The six month period for certiorari indicated, until 1978, the degree of dispatch that was required, and we invite views as to the operation of the shorter period.

4.31   There are benefits in having a uniform approach to time limits for all the remedies available by way of judicial review, and we would regard it as retrograde to distinguish between remedies as regards the degree of speed necessary to invoke their use. On the other hand, we can see that in some circumstances the imperative for speed may be of an entirely different order in different contexts, and that

---

[45]   See section 14 below. Cf. C.Lewis, "The Exhaustion of Alternative Remedies in Administrative law", [1992] C.L.J. 138, 143.

[46]   See the comments referred to above at para. 4.5.

accordingly the element of discretion forms an important part of the balancing of these competing interests.

4.32   The question whether delay within the stated time limit should either bar leave or the grant of relief depends, in our view, on the length of the time limit. If the current three month period is to be retained, we provisionally consider that delay within that period should be disregarded, except possibly where substantial hardship, prejudice, etc. is proved. This might, in effect, place an onus on respondents to take the issue at the leave stage, if they so wished, rather than leaving it to the court to consider on an ex parte basis. It would be incumbent on a respondent to particularise the hardship and detriment relevant to the situation to which the application relates. On the other hand, if a longer period of six months were to be adopted, the case for excluding considerations of delay from the court's decision as to whether to grant leave or to grant the remedy, would be weaker.

4.33   Whatever view is adopted concerning the factor of delay within the time limit period, we consider that the power to extend time after the period should be retained as at present.

THE LEAVE STAGE

Background

5.1   Order 53, rule 3(1) provides that no application can be made for judicial review
         without obtaining the leave of the court. The application must be made ex parte
         to a judge, together with the appropriate papers, identifying the relief sought and
         the grounds. Many applications are determined on the papers without need for an
         oral hearing, although that is an option available to the applicant. Renewal of a
         refused application and appeal from the refusal of leave depends to some extent on
         whether it is a criminal cause or matter, and these issues are covered in section 12
         of this paper. The Commission's 1976 Report recommended the retention of the
         requirement of leave.[1]

5.2   The explicit purpose of the leave stage is to filter out hopeless applications for
         judicial review. Ill-founded applications delay finality in decision making: they
         exploit and exacerbate delays within the judicial system and are detrimental to the
         progress of well founded legal challenges. While this is generally true of litigation,
         in the case of applications challenging regulations and decisions the public policy
         factors set out at paragraphs 2.1-2.7 have been seen as justifying a leave
         requirement. In its 1971 Working Paper the Commission stated that the likelihood
         of frivolous actions to challenge an administrative act or order might be increased
         by the fact that anyone adversely affected will have standing to challenge it and it
         was therefore "all the more important to have some procedure for striking down
         applications without delay and cost for the particular public authorities and
         tribunals concerned".[2] Support for the need for a leave requirement has been
         expressly voiced by the higher judiciary, particularly Lord Woolf, and was
         originally introduced following the Hanworth Committee's Third Report of the
         Business of the Courts.[3]

5.3   In *R. v. Secretary of State for the Home Department, ex parte Doorga*[4], Lord
         Donaldson M.R. identified three categories of cases: first, cases where there are
         prima facie reasons for granting judicial review - here leave should be granted;

---

[1]   Report on Remedies in Administrative Law (1976), Law Com., No.73 paras. 37-39.

[2]   Remedies in Administrative Law (1971), Working Paper No. 40, para. 98.

[3]   (1936), Cmd. 5066.

[4]   [1990] C.O.D. 109, 110.

second, cases that are wholly unarguable - where leave should be refused; third, an intermediate category, where either there is no prima facie case but there is cause for concern to know more about the position, or alternatively, the feeling that there may be an easy answer dealing with the case. In this intermediate category, Lord Donaldson proposed that it would be reasonable for a judge to adjourn the application to allow an opportunity for inter partes hearing[5] and we consider the question of whether, in suitable cases, the court should have power to give interim relief prior to the granting of leave below.[6]

5.4   A recent survey[7] has looked at the way in which the leave requirement works in practice. It found that the majority of cases were determined on the "quick look" approach; but that a sizeable minority were subjected to what might be called a "good look", with more consideration of the merits of the application and going beyond the issue of whether the application was arguable.

Issues

5.5   Criticisms of the leave requirement centre around the principle of having a leave hurdle at all and the manner in which the judiciary apply the procedure. The JUSTICE-All Souls Report drew a comparison with the assertion of private law rights by citizen, and argued that the citizen should not have to obtain leave in order to proceed against the state or other administrative bodies.[8] Craig[9] has argued that public law (i.e. not just private law) may give rise to substantive rights justifying a right to take legal proceedings. He argues that prior to the reforms in 1977 and even until *O'Reilly* v. *Mackman*, proceedings brought by way of injunction or for declarations were viewed as substantive rights which were not subject to a leave requirement. An unfettered right to start proceedings has been rendered conditional.

5.6   More pragmatic criticisms[10] suggest that the leave procedure is unnecessary. Furthermore, some important principles of law have emerged from cases in which

---

[5]   See also, *R. v. Secretary of State for the Home Department, ex p. Begum* [1990] C.O.D. 107, 108.

[6]   Paras. 6.32 - 33.

[7]   A.P. Le Sueur and M.Sunkin, "Applications for Judicial Review: The Requirement of Leave", [1992] P.L. 102.

[8]   *Op. cit.*, p.153, para. 6.23.

[9]   P.P.Craig, "English Administrative Law - Procedures, Rights and Remedies", (1990) 2 E.R.P.L. 425, 436,437, 440.

[10]   A.P. Le Sueur and M.Sunkin, *op. cit.*, 105, 106.

leave was initially refused.[11] The JUSTICE-All Souls Report considered that, as delay and workload problems are a problem in all parts of the judicial system, it is not equitable to discriminate against public law applications by the use of a leave requirement.[12]

5.7 The currently available judicial statistics on judicial review, and the grant of leave, are in some respects problematical, as they do not identify the reasons why some applications are withdrawn. However, given the very significant proportion of applications which are rejected or withdrawn,[13] the leave stage, regarded as a period in the life of a case, as distinct from the leave requirement *per se* undoubtedly has a very significant effect on filtering out cases. It is the growing numbers of applications which has fuelled judicial fears that the courts are being increasingly swamped by cases.

Options for reform

5.8 The alternative which is most often canvassed[14] to having a leave stage at all, is that the court should simply use its inherent powers to strike out claims that are frivolous, vexatious or otherwise an abuse of the process of the court.[15] The application of that test would, however, involve respondents being put to the expense of getting a case struck out but, more importantly, its stringency would lead to very few applications being struck out at that stage. Any modification to the strike out procedure to reflect the policy factors would involve the risk of replicating, in a more confusing form, the existing procedure.

5.9 If it is thought that a leave requirement is right in principle, consideration could be given to remedying the particular aspects of procedure which have provoked concern. For example, it might be preferable for the rules to reflect the procedure

---

[11]   e.g. R. v. *Medical Appeal Tribunal, ex p. Gilmore* [1957] 1 Q.B. 574; *R.* v. *Panel on Take-overs and Mergers, ex p. Datafin Plc.* [1987] Q.B. 815.

[12]   Op. cit. para. 6.25.

[13]   *Judicial Statistics, Annual Report, 1990-1991*, indicate that of the 2089 applications for leave to move for judicial review received, 923 were allowed and 929 refused (the shortfall representing cases not disposed of at the end of the year). For the figures between 1971-1975 see Law Com. No. 73, paras. 37-38.

[14]   For instance, by the JUSTICE-All Souls Report, p.153, para. 6.25, and H.W.R. Wade, *Administrative Law* (6th ed., 1988), p. 680. See also H.W.R. Wade, "Procedure and Prerogative in Public Law", (1985) 101 L.Q.R. 180, 189-190 for the suggestion that the need for speed and other requirements when challenging the exercise of statutory powers might be recognised under one single form of procedure.

[15]   R.S.C., Order 18, rule 19.

adopted in the intermediate category of cases in which the court needs input from the respondent before determining the ex parte application.

5.10   If respondents were to be more involved in the decision as to the granting of leave, detailed consideration would need to be given as to how such participation could better fulfil the desire to ensure that the correct decision is made, whilst not elaborating the procedure to an extent that is counter-productive.

5.11   We invite views developing the following suggestion. The Crown Office and the nominated judges might adopt a practice whereby all applications, once complete are placed before a nominated judge within a specified period after they are lodged and are determined on paper within a specified period after they are placed before him. (Slightly longer periods might be prescribed for the law vacations). In those cases in the intermediate category identified by Lord Donaldson[16] the judge would direct an oral hearing and direct that the proposed respondents be served with the papers and allowed a specified period from the date of service in which they might write to the Crown Office and to the applicants setting out their views on the application and attaching copies of any relevant documents. A date for the oral hearing should be set as soon as the judge has directed on oral hearing, but it should be understood that there is no need for the proposed respondents to be represented at the hearing and except in exceptional cases they are unlikely to be awarded their costs of attending what is in form an ex parte hearing. Similar arrangements should be made by the Crown Office in those cases in which the applicant applies for an oral hearing when he lodges the application. This might, in certain situations, be more advantageous and expeditious than the present practice where the respondent is invited to appear to oppose the ex parte application. Whereas the opposed ex parte procedure may have value, it currently operates outside the provisions of Order 53, and it has been criticised by the Administrative Law Bar Association as generating expense.

5.12   There have also been suggestions aimed at achieving a greater degree of certainty and uniformity in the way in which courts exercise the discretion to grant or refuse leave. Le Sueur and Sunkin suggest the introduction of a comprehensive statement of grounds for refusing leave and the introduction of a requirement to state the reasons for refusing leave.

5.13   It has also been suggested[17] that there should be a power to dispense with the leave stage where both parties agree that there is a serious issue to be tried.

---

[16]   See paragraph 5.3.

[17]   A.P. Le Sueur and M.Sunkin, *op cit.*. See also Remedies in Administrative Law (1971), Working Paper No. 40, para. 100. But cf. *R.* v. *Durham C.C., ex p. Robinson, The Times,* 31 January 1992.

Provisional View

5.14   Whilst we tend to accept that a leave stage is necessary, we consider that there are ways in which the procedure might be improved. We refer below to complaints as to the costs and inconvenience which sometimes arise caused by the ex parte nature of the leave procedure.[18] We have also noted above Lord Donaldson's comments on the intermediate category of cases in which an adjournment of the leave application to hear the other side may be appropriate. This is a matter for which the rules do not currently provide, and if it is to continue the arrangements for it may need to be formalised.

---

[18]   See section 11.

Background

6.1   Two issues arise. First, the availability of interim relief against the Crown, and second whether, in judicial review proceedings, the court should be empowered to order interim relief before leave is granted. In the Commission's 1976 Report, it was generally accepted that no interim relief could be granted against the Crown or Crown servants[1], but the Commission recommended that courts should be empowered to declare the terms of an interim injunction which it would otherwise have granted, but for the Crown's special position.[2]   This particular recommendation was left unimplemented.   The present position has to be interpreted by reference to R.S.C. Order 53, rule 3 (10) (a) and (b) and section 31(2) of the 1981 Act.[3] These provisions also make it clear that it is a precondition to the ordering of interim relief that leave to apply for judicial review has been granted.

Interim Injunctions : Domestic law

6.2   The general view as to why, in domestic law, there is no power to grant interim injunctive relief against the Crown is that there is no jurisdiction to grant an injunction against the Crown; i.e. without power to grant the substantive remedy, there is no power to grant that relief as an interim measure.[4] Although the Crown Proceedings Act 1947 widened the power to make orders against the Crown and to declare the rights of the parties (though not to grant an injunction) section 21(2) only applies to civil proceedings. Crown side proceedings, which includes judicial review, are not civil proceedings.

6.3   However, it was thought that the enactment of section 31(2) and the revised Order 53, rule 3(10) had given courts power to grant injunctions (and hence interim injunctions) against officers of the Crown, and against government ministers acting

---

[1]   Law Com. No. 73, paras. 23 and 29. It has always been clear that relief can be obtained against other public authorities such as local authorities.

[2]   Law Com. No. 73, para. 59(i).

[3]   See Annex 1.

[4]   For a defence of the present position, see Sir John Laws in M.Supperstone Q.C. and J.Goudie Q.C., *Judicial Review* (1992), pp. 253-258.

under statutory powers in their own name, though not against the Crown itself.[5] The liability of government ministers acting in their own name was seen as analogous to their long established liability to prerogative orders of mandamus and prohibition.[6]

6.4   In *R. v. Secretary of State for Transport, ex parte Factortame Ltd.* (hereafter called *"Factortame (No.1)"*),[7] the House of Lords held that the court had no power to grant an interim injunction against a Minister of the Crown. Lord Bridge (with whom all their Lordships agreed) disagreed with the developing consensus that section 31(2) had altered the position of the Crown. Although Lord Bridge's reasoning in relation to the interpretation of section 31(2) is debatable and the decision has been criticised,[8] it must be taken to have settled the matter as far as domestic law is concerned.

Interim Injunctions: EC law

6.5   The House of Lords, in the course of *Factortame (No. 1)* requested a preliminary ruling from the European Court of Justice under Article 177 to determine whether as a matter of Community law, a national court has jurisdiction to grant an interim order against the Crown to protect rights claimed under EC law. One of the grounds on which the legality of the statute and regulations regarding the registration of fishing vessels[9] were challenged was that they infringed the EC Treaty and deprived the applicants of enforceable Community rights. The European Court of Justice stated[10] that the principle of full effectiveness of community law required the national court to set aside any rule of national law which prevented it from granting interim relief which ought otherwise to be

---

[5]   *R. v. Secretary of State for the Home Department, ex p. Herbage* [1987] Q.B. 872. See also *R. v. Licensing Authority, ex p. Smith Kline (No. 2)* [1990] 1 Q.B. 574. See further G.Aldous and J.Alder, *Applications for Judicial Review* (1985), 42-3, 70-1; R.G.F. Gordon, *Judicial Review: Law and Procedure* (1985), para. 5-09; C.T.Emery and B.Smythe, *Judicial Review: Legal Limits of Official Power* (1986), pp. 295-6. See, in relation to government ministers acting in their own name, H.W.R. Wade, *Administrative Law* (6th ed., 1988), p.589.

[6]   *Padfield* v. *Minister of Agriculture, Fisheries and Food* [1968] A.C. 997.

[7]   [1990] 2 A.C. 85.

[8]   J.Hanna, "Community Rights All at Sea", (1990) 106 L.Q.R. 2; H.W.R. Wade, "Injunctive Relief against the Crown and Ministers", (1991) 107 L.Q.R. 4.

[9]   Merchant Shipping Act 1988 and the Merchant Shipping (Registration of Fishing Vessels) Regulations 1988, S.I. 1988, No. 1926.

[10]   In *Factortame (No. 2)* (Case C 213/89), [1991] 1 A.C. 603,644.

available. The House of Lords[11] granted an interim injunction against the Secretary of State restraining, in effect, application of the Act and regulations to the registration of the applicants' vessels.

6.6   The position now therefore, is that there is a two tier system regarding interim injunctive relief against the Crown and Crown officers. Where Community rights are involved (even only putative rights), the courts have jurisdiction to grant an interim injunction against the Crown and also to disapply an Act of Parliament. But in domestic law, *Factortame (No.1)* rules out any such interim injunction. The position is clearly anomalous, and has been criticised by Lord Donaldson M.R. as being wrong in principle.[12]

Interim Declarations

6.7   An alternative approach to interim relief which has been considered before (and by the Law Commission as mentioned earlier) is that of the interim declaration. It is clear that in English law the authorities prevent anything in the nature of an interim declaratory order. Such an order has been said to be illogical.[13] There have been academic criticisms of this narrow concept of declaratory relief,[14] and the reasoning in English authorities was rejected in proceedings before the Supreme Court of Israel in *Yotvin* v. *The State of Israel*,[15] where Cohn J. stated that he

> "failed to find any logical or legal contradiction between the declaration of a certain right or obligation and the temporary nature of such declaration: the meaning of the impermanence is that the declaration refers to a right or obligation that exists prima facie; in making a merely interim declaration, the judge reserves his right and admits his obligation to re-examine it after a full hearing at the trial."

Stay of Proceedings

6.8   Different views have been taken as to the power to grant a stay against the decision

---

[11]   [1991] 1 A.C. 603.

[12]   *M.* v. *Home Office* [1992] Q.B. 270, 306H-307A.

[13]   *International General Electric Company of New York Ltd.* v. *Commissioners of Customs and Excise* [1962] Ch. 784, 790; *R.* v. *Inland Revenue Commissioners, ex p. Rossminster Ltd.* [1980] A.C. 952, 1027.

[14]   I.Zamir, "The Declaratory Judgement Revisited", [1977] C.L.P. 43, 51-52. See also I.Zamir, *The Declaratory Judgment* (1962), pp. 309-311; P.P.Craig, *Administrative Law* (2nd ed., 1989), pp. 527-528.

[15]   1979 (Cohn, Shamgar, Barak JJ.).

of a Minister.[16] *R. v. Secretary of State for Education and Science, ex parte Avon County Council*[17] raised the issue of the meaning of a stay of proceedings, and its possible utility, as a remedy which avoids the inability of courts to grant an interim injunction against the Crown. In *Avon*, it was held that a stay could be granted against a Minister of the Crown and that the proceedings which were capable of being stayed extended not only to court proceedings, but included a decision and the decision-making process of an officer or Minister of the Crown.[18]

6.9   However, doubt has been cast on the approach taken in *Avon* by *Minister of Foreign Affairs* v. *Vehicles and Supplies Ltd*. Lord Oliver said that a stay

" ... is not an order enforceable by proceedings for contempt because it is not, in its nature, capable of being 'breached' by a party to the proceedings or anyone else. It simply means that the relevant court or tribunal cannot, whilst the stay endures, effectively entertain any further proceedings".[19]

6.10   Lord Oliver's approach is reflected in the manner in which stays of proceedings have been formulated in the judgments and orders of the High Court.[20] Where, in order to give effect to the stay, the court considers it is necessary to require anyone to do or abstain from doing an act, this is effected by the addition of a further order in the nature of an injunction. The element of restraint is not implicit in the stay itself; it is an additional provision.

6.11   There are difficulties in defining the proper scope of proceedings that can be stayed by reference to the completeness of the decision and whether it has been implemented. It may be particularly artificial to separate these stages where the

---

[16]   *R. v. Secretary of State for the Home Department, ex p. Kirkwood* [1984] 1 W.L.R. 913; *R. v. Secretary of State for the Home Department, ex p. Mohammed Yaqoob* [1984] 1 W.L.R. 920; *R. v. Licensing Authority, ex p. Smith Kline and French Laboratories Ltd. (No. 2)* [1990] 1 Q.B. 574, 596, 602, 604.

[17]   [1991] 1 Q.B. 558, 560-2.

[18]   [1991] 1 Q.B. 558, 561F-562D (C.A.).

[19]   [1991] 1 W.L.R. 550, 556F (P.C., Jamaica), the decision which shortly preceded *Avon*. See also *R. v. Secretary of State for the Home Department, ex p. Muboyayi* [1992] Q.B. 244 where, although Glidewell L.J. agreed that doubt had been cast on *Avon*, Taylor L.J. adhered to its correctness and Lord Donaldson M.R. expressed no opinion.

[20]   See, for example, *Daniell's Chancery Forms* (6th ed., 1914) pp. 1066-1072 and *Seton's Judgments and Orders*, (7th ed., 1912), vol.I, pp. 130 - 133.

decision and its implementation are the responsibility of the same Minister or officer of the Crown.[21]

6.12 The power to grant a stay of the proceedings to which the application for judicial review relates is referred to in Order 53, rule 3(10). In *Smith Kline (No. 2)* Dillon L.J. took the view that the meaning of "proceedings" in Order 53, rule 3(10)(a) (and which is also implicitly applicable in rule 3(10)(b)) has expanded to accommodate the expansion in the types of matters which are liable to judicial review.[22] In this way, it may be suggested that the use of the term "proceedings" has been significantly expanded by changes in the substantive scope of judicial review.

Principles on which interim relief granted[23]

6.13 The tests generally applicable when a court is considering whether to grant interlocutory injunctions are those enunciated in *American Cyanamid Co. v. Ethicon Ltd.*[24] The extent to which they required modification where relief is sought against a public authority was first considered in cases involving local authorities.[25] In *Factortame (No. 2)*, the House of Lords considered the tests where relief is sought against the Crown. Lord Goff stated that the court had first to consider the availability to either side of an adequate remedy in damages. As public authorities are not generally liable in damages in respect of ultra vires acts,[26] this element of the *American Cyanamid* test did not provide much assistance in public law cases. As regards the balance of convenience, the court had to look more widely, taking account of the public in general to whom an authority owed duties. When exercising its discretion, Lord Goff considered that

"... the court should not restrain a public authority by interim injunction from enforcing an apparently authentic law unless it is satisfied, having regard to all the circumstances, that the challenge to the validity of the law

---

21 See *R.* v. *Secretary of State for the Home Department, ex p. Muboyayi* [1992] Q.B. 244.

22 [1990] 1 Q.B. 574, 596.

23 See, generally, M.H.Matthews, "Injunctions, Interim Relief and Proceedings against Crown Servants", (1988) 8 O.J.L.S. 154, 163-168.

24 [1975] A.C. 396

25 *Smith v. I.L.E.A.* [1978] 1 All E.R. 411; *Meade v. Haringey L.B.C.* [1979] 1 W.L.R. 637.

26 *Bourgoin S.A. v. Ministry of Agriculture Fisheries and Food* [1986] Q.B. 716; *R. v. Knowlsey B.C., ex p. Maguire* (1992) 142 N.L.J. 1375.

is, prima facie, so firmly based as to justify so exceptional a course being taken."[27]

The Case for Reform: the Position of the Crown

6.14   Where the issue before the court relates to protection of the citizen against unauthorised governmental action, the court needs, as in any other form of litigation, to have adequate powers to maintain the interim position and to avoid irreparable harm. Case law involving public authority respondents, and Crown and Crown officer respondents in EC related cases, has helped to develop principles taking account of the wider public interest and obligations of the respondents.

6.15   Given the unavailability of monetary compensation in respect of ultra vires acts, it is particularly important that the court should be able to grant interim protection. The Crown, and now local authorities charged with enforcing the law,[28] will not be required to give an undertaking to pay damages if it subsequently transpires that an interim injunction to restrain a breach of the law should not have been granted. In any event the possibility of recovering damages is remote.[29] The absence of interlocutory relief against the Crown and its officers has been said to be "a serious procedural defect in the English system of administrative law".[30]

6.16   The arguments against the grant of interim relief against the Crown in domestic cases may similarly be reviewed.

6.17   First, there is a necessary presumption of validity in favour of the decisions taken by the Crown and its officers which should be maintained until shown to be wrong. By granting interim relief, the court would interrupt the carrying out of the duties imposed on the authority, casting doubt on that presumption of validity and overstepping the boundary between adjudication and administration before the issue of the validity of what has been done has been properly determined.[31]

6.18   Second, there is a need for the administration to act swiftly if necessary without fear of inappropriate judicial intervention.

---

27   [1991] 1 A.C. 603, at p. 674D.

28   *Kirklees M.B.C.* v. *Wickes Building Supplies Ltd.* [1992] 3 W.L.R. 170, (H.L.).

29   Note, however, that in cases involving EC law, this may be less remote. See further para. 1.5 above.

30   *R.* v. *Inland Revenue Commissioners, ex p. Rossminster Ltd.* [1980] A.C. 952, 1014H (*per* Lord Diplock).

31   *Ibid.* [1980] A.C. 952, 1001, 1027.

6.19   Third, injunctive relief ought generally not to be ordered if the parties are willing to undertake to maintain the status quo pending the full trial.[32] The Crown and its officers will generally give and will honour, such undertakings. The use of compulsion, where consensus is available, is inappropriate.

6.20   The courts are traditionally reluctant to make orders which they cannot enforce. This is particularly relevant in the field of discretionary remedies, whether for specific performance or, injunctive relief, or otherwise. The scope for enforcing an order against the Crown is restricted. If the reality is that the court must depend on consensual compliance, that ought to be reflected in the nature of the directions it gives.

6.21   Against these arguments it may be said that the presumption of validity applies to the activities of other public authorities which do not claim and are not protected against the making of interim orders.[33] The need for swift action in emergencies is no argument against the need for the availability of interim protection in non-urgent situations and ignores the discretionary nature of such interim relief. The ability of the Crown to give undertakings which reflect the possibly dubious validity of acts which it has previously executed removes much of the force from the argument that the court should not grant interim relief for a similar precautionary purpose. Orders of mandamus and prohibition have been made against Ministers and the Crown is (to some extent, namely in the form of its Ministers and servants) subject to the contempt jurisdiction (*M. v. Home Office*[34]) and to habeas corpus, so there is precedent to that extent for acknowledging the Crown's liability to injunctions if enforcement is entailed.

Options for reform

6.22   In approaching reform, it is necessary to determine whether reform should be aimed solely at the protection of the interim position, by the development of some form of interim relief, or whether the issue goes to the power to grant final injunctions against the Crown, or its Ministers and officers. *Factortame (No. 1)* relates to the lack of jurisdiction of the courts to grant any injunction, final or interlocutory, against the Crown, or its Ministers or officers. If the inability of the court to grant final relief by way of injunction were to be reversed, the interim position would automatically shift to enable interlocutory injunctions to be granted, by operation of Order 53, rule 3(10)(b).

---

[32]   As in *M. v. Home Office* [1992] 1 Q.B. 270.

[33]   M.H.Matthews, "Injunctions, Interim Relief and Proceedings against Crown Servants", (1988) 8 O.J.L.S. 154, 156.

[34]   [1992] 1 Q.B. 270. An appeal to the House of Lords is pending in this case.

6.23   On the other hand, if the perceived problem is more specifically in relation to the need for effective interim measures whilst the court exercises its jurisdiction, it may be that reform ought to concentrate on reform of the interim protection which can be secured, not on widening the forms of final relief to which the Crown is to be subjected.

6.24   Whilst the concept of a stay on proceedings is relatively easy to grasp in relation to staying the implementation by a Minister of a decision which he or she has taken, or the staying of enforcement proceedings, the concept of staying regulations on an interim basis, whilst their legality is disputed, is unfamiliar and may appear less appropriate. What is needed is a signal from the court which alerts not only the parties but all who are potentially affected by the disputed decision, regulations etc., that proceedings are pending to challenge the validity of the regulations, etc.. Some mechanism is needed which effectively places a hold on the operation of the disputed regulations, until the proceedings are fully heard.

6.25   The benefits of using an interim declaration[35] to cover this situation are that it provides a public statement which will become known to all who might otherwise continue to apply the disputed regulations. Whilst it might be said that the granting of a declaration in an interim form inappropriately suggests that the court has already made up its mind as to the likely grant of final relief, it could be argued that this is beneficial. The principles relevant to the grant of interim relief are that it is only granted where strong prima facie grounds exist, and it might be argued that an indication of the likelihood that final relief will be granted is preferable to a form of relief, such as a stay, which does not do so.

6.26   We have outlined above the nature of the possible interim remedies. The main options are:

(a)   Enabling courts to grant injunctions against the responsible Minister or a designated official of the Crown - often referred to as the persona designata method - in domestic cases rather than against the Crown as such as they do in EC cases. This approach reflects the attempts before *Factortame (No. 1)* to achieve a solution that did not require legislation.[36] If it is thought that reform must address the ability of the court to grant relief in the form of injunctions, whether finally or as an interim measure, this would be a possible option.

---

[35]   The Commission's own preference in 1976 was to develop the role of the interim declaration.

[36]   See para. 6.3 above.

(b)   Reform of section 21 of the Crown Proceedings Act 1947, so as to include Crown side proceedings in the scope of those proceedings in respect of which the court is empowered to make orders. This too would address both the expansion of forms of relief and interim protection available to the court.

(c)   Development of the use of interim declarations. This would more specifically target the need for interim protection, without the overtones of compulsion.

(d)   Development of the grant of stays in proceedings against the Crown, or its Ministers and officers. This too would target the interim protection, without overt compulsion and without the implicit creation of a new form of substantive relief.

6.27   In considering the relative merits of injunctions on the one hand and stays and interim declarations on the other, as a solution to the problem of providing an appropriate interim measure addressed to the Crown and its Ministers, the latter:-

(a)   specifically address the interim position, which is the problem area, without creating a new form of final remedy;

(b)   are compatible with the nature of the prerogative jurisdiction, taking account as it does of the public interest;

(c)   ensure that the court's discretion at the final hearing is not pre-empted, so that it is then able either to grant an effective remedy, or to decide that there should be no relief.

6.28   As between stays and interim declarations, whilst the arguments currently being employed in favour of granting stays of decisions of Ministers are debatable, a stay:-

(a)   accords with the form in which interim relief has hitherto been granted in prerogative proceedings, and

(b)   treats all public authorities in a similar way, not distinguishing between the Crown and other public authorities.

6.29   In view of the doubts that have been expressed about stays in their present form,[37] if they are to be used it would be important to formulate any new statutory power to grant stays in a way which embraced more clearly than do the current provisions and rules, the decision making and implementing process to which it is intended

---

[37]   See paras. 6.9 -6.11 above.

45

that it should properly apply, rather than limit its application to proceedings before a court.

Provisional View

6.30   Our provisional view is that the Crown's continued immunity from interim relief is not sustainable on grounds of legal principle. We, like our predecessors in 1976, are not convinced by the legal arguments for continuing to protect the special position of the Crown. The case for interim relief in domestic proceedings has strengthened in the light of the decision of the House of Lords in *Factortame (No. 2)*. We favour reform which would eliminate the anomalies between the position of the Crown and other public authorities and between the approach to be adopted in domestic and EC cases.

6.31   The essential element in reform is to ensure that the court has adequate power to protect the interim position. The options most specifically aimed at the effective protection by the court of the interim position, are those involving a statutory power to stay, pending determination of the review proceedings and a power to make an interim declaration. We would welcome views on the relative preference between formulating such interim protection in terms of a stay, or a grant of an interim declaration, where the nature of the stay is such as will affect persons other than the parties to the proceedings, and in particular where what is in issue is the legality of regulations of wide general impact.

The Case for Reform: interim relief prior to the granting of leave

6.32   The inability of the court in judicial review proceedings to grant an injunction, or order a stay, until it has granted leave, has been said to lead to practical difficulties. A judge may not have time or the proper material to reach a decision as to whether the case for judicial review is arguable but unless it is possible to stay executive action, to provide an opportunity to decide whether to grant leave, irremediable injustice may be done. For instance, the application for leave may come before the court only hours before the applicant is about to be evicted from a house or deported.

6.33   Although similar difficulties can arise in other types of ex parte interlocutory applications made before proceedings are commenced, it is only in judicial review that the leave of the court is a condition of commencing proceedings. In private law proceedings, in an emergency an ex parte injunction can be granted on an undertaking to issue a writ. In judicial review proceedings leave should not be granted on inadequate material and until leave is granted, there is no power to order interim relief. In some such cases applicants and the court may seek to preserve the status quo by using habeas corpus but the scope of that remedy is

46

limited and it is debatable whether it is appropriate.[38] We seek the views of consultees as to whether the power to order interim relief pending the determination of the leave proceedings, would be useful and if so, in what circumstances and subject to what safeguards.

---

[38]   See Section 7.

INTERRELATIONSHIP BETWEEN HABEAS CORPUS AND JUDICIAL REVIEW

Background

7.1 The interrelationship between these two routes of challenge to the legality of a detention is revealed in particular in two very different contexts, immigration and mental health. The Mental Health Review Tribunal does not have jurisdiction to consider the legality of an application for admission to hospital for treatment.[1] The only means of challenge available are by way of habeas corpus[2] and judicial review. Where the writ of habeas corpus is sought the detainer has to give cause for the detention. In the context of hospital admissions the courts have been reluctant to go behind the apparent validity of the authorising documents in order to investigate compliance with the procedures prescribed in the statute.[3]

7.2 However, in habeas corpus proceedings relating to both mental health and immigration applicants have sought to widen the scope of the court's investigation into the issues so as to raise grounds of challenge similar to those available in judicial review. But in *R. v. Secretary of State for the Home Department ex p. Muboyayi*[4] the Court held that where the applicant was not challenging a precedent fact on which his or her detention was based, then unless and until that administrative decision was impugned by judicial review, an application for habeas corpus could not succeed.[5]

7.3 Lord Donaldson M.R. stated, further, that an application for habeas corpus alone would be insufficient to raise all the considerations which an applicant would need to argue in order to impugn the administrative decision complained of. In order to quash a decision to refuse entry to an immigrant the court needed to be working within the framework of an application for judicial review together with its in-built

---

[1] *Ex parte Waldron* [1986] Q.B. 824, 846B-C, F-G.

[2] R.S.C., Order 54.

[3] *R. v. The Governor of Broadmoor, ex parte Argles* 28 June 1974 noted in B.M. Hoggett, *Mental Health Law* (3rd., 1990), p. 255. For a less restrictive view see *R. v. Board of Control, ex p. Rutty* [1956] 2 Q.B. 109.

[4] [1992] Q.B. 244.

[5] A similar question as to the scope of habeas corpus applications in the mental health context was raised but not answered in *Perkins* v. *Bath District Health Authority*; *R.* v. *Wessex Mental Health Review Tribunal, ex p. Wiltshire C.C.*, *The Times*, 29 August 1989.

safeguards. Whereas the House of Lords' decision in *Khawaja*[6] had emphasised the common principles applicable to habeas corpus and judicial review where the liberty of the subject was in issue, in *Muboyayi*, Taylor L.J. said that *Khawaja* did not extend the scope of the court's enquiry on a habeas application beyond objective precedent facts to matters of judgment. If matters of judgment were excluded, then issues relevant to the exercise of that judgment (other than precedent facts) were not relevant.

Issues

7.4   Although it may appear that attempts to bring grounds familiar in judicial review proceedings to bear in habeas corpus actions are aimed at circumventing the procedural restrictions of Ord 53, which raises questions about the balance of private and public interest, the real reason for applicants pursuing this course is the delay they face, of 17 months on average, between the grant of leave and the substantive hearing in judicial review proceedings, unless expedition is ordered. This delay often means that events supersede the legal issue (typically the release of a patient on other grounds or the return of a would-be immigrant to a country, which he is then unable to leave again), making the issue academic and therefore leading the court to dismiss the case. We invite views as to how this difficulty might be addressed, or whether it is simply a consequence of the pressure of the increased caseload.[7]

7.5   In *Muboyayi*, the court considered the potential for using concurrent applications for both habeas corpus and judicial review to ensure effective interim protection.[8] As we have seen, in judicial review proceedings no interim protection can be given prior to the granting of leave. However, the effectiveness of habeas corpus as a means of providing interim relief is open to question. First, it seems clear from the cases considered above that the courts are not prepared to go far beyond assessing the prima facie legality of the documents and the objective precedent facts in habeas corpus applications. Second, if on an application for habeas corpus the detention is declared to be unlawful there will be nothing left to review by way Order 53. A potentially reviewable decision would have been in effect quashed. The writ of habeas corpus operates more like an application for a declaration of no cause of action than as a form of interim relief.

---

6   *R.* v. *Secretary of State for the Home Department, ex p. Khawaja* [1984] A.C. 74.

7   One possibility, on which see section 2 above, is that the court might make an advisory declaration in this type of situation.

8   See also the dicta of Lord Donaldson in *M* v. *Home Office* [1992] 1 Q.B. 270, 293G. The same reasoning would apply to the use of habeas corpus in the mental health context.

7.6   Impetus for reform of the procedure for habeas corpus comes from a growing realisation of the disparity between the procedures used for habeas corpus and judicial review limitations.   On the various occasions when the prerogative remedies have been reformed, to develop the remedies and safeguards in the public interest, habeas corpus has been left virtually unchanged, partly perhaps because of the weight of its historical and constitutional importance, and partly because of its very limited role of application.[9]

Options for reform

7.7   In the light of the developments in judicial review and the apparent increase in the use of habeas corpus we invite consultees' views on whether some rationalisation and simplification of the various procedures in Order 54 would be desirable but which would also leave the traditional constitutional role of habeas corpus unaltered.

7.8   As regards the apparent insufficiency of habeas corpus to address properly issues which would be examined on judicial review, there may be scope for reform of the Order 53 procedure, which would meet the needs of applicants who are currently attempting to press-gang habeas corpus into wider service, whilst at the same time preserving the function of habeas corpus as a safeguard against plainly illegal detention. A new form of interim relief could be made available at the leave stage to allow a detainee who could show strong prima facie grounds of illegality (under Order 53 grounds of review), to be released, pending the full hearing.[10] This would enable the courts to look further than they do at present behind the validity of the documents authorising a detention, without being put in the position of being asked in effect, to quash, finally a reviewable decision.

---

[9]   Remedies in Administrative Law (1971), Working Paper No. 40, paras. 152-153.

[10]   Where the Crown is the respondent this suggestion is necessarily conditional upon the possibility of interim relief being available at all. See Section 6.

50

Background

8.1   The criterion for ordering discovery, set out in R.S.C., Order 24, rule 13(1), is that the court must be of the opinion that the order is necessary either for disposing fairly of the cause or for saving costs. The principles applicable to discovery and cross-examination on affidavit, are regarded by the courts as common to all proceedings, and are summed up in the phrase, "where the court believes that it is necessary in order that justice may be done between the parties".

8.2   The remedying of previous procedural disadvantages, in particular lack of discovery, was an important part of the justification for the introduction of the requirement of exclusivity in *O'Reilly* v. *Mackman*.[11] Lord Diplock emphasised the common approach to granting discovery adopted by the courts in all proceedings, stating that any differences in practice would be related to the different nature of the issues normally arising.[12]

8.3   The fact that the courts are adopting, in the context of public law remedies, a different and more cautious approach to granting discovery has been overtly acknowledged.[13] In contrast with the approach applied in civil litigation, where automatic discovery is the norm, in judicial review the court consciously scrutinises the strength of the applicant's case before granting discovery. More particularly, where the Crown is the respondent, the absence of automatic discovery against the Crown leads both the respondent body and the court to scrutinise more closely any application for discovery.

8.4   In *R.* v. *Inland Revenue Commissioners, ex p. National Federation of Self-Employed and Small Businesses*,[14] (hereafter called "the *National Federation of Self-Employed*" case) Lord Scarman appeared to introduce a requirement of prima facie breach of public duty before ordering discovery, saying

"Upon general principles, discovery should not be ordered unless and until the court is satisfied that the evidence reveals reasonable grounds for believing that there has been a breach of public duty: and it should be

---

[11]   [1983] 2 A.C. 237, 280-282, (*per* Lord Diplock).

[12]   *Ibid.*, 282E-G.

[13]   Sir Harry Woolf, "Public Law - Private Law: Why the Divide? A Personal View", [1986] P.L. 220, 231.

[14]   [1982] A.C. 617, 654E-F.

limited strictly to documents relevant to the issue which emerges from the affidavits."

Lord Wilberforce, in the same case, dealing with the situation on the more general principle of preventing abuse of discovery for the purposes of fishing for evidence, said

> "... if as I think, the case against the revenue does not, on the evidence, leave the ground, no court, in my opinion, would consider ordering discovery against the revenue in the hope of eliciting some impropriety."[15]

8.5   A further distinct test applicable in judicial review and not in civil proceedings is that the court will only grant discovery in judicial review proceedings if there is something on the face of the affidavit or the record which suggests that the evidence is unsatisfactory or inaccurate.[16] Since it is often the case that the only evidence that will enable the accuracy of an affidavit setting out the basis of a decision to be challenged is in the hands of the respondent, in practice this constitutes an important limitation on discovery in judicial review proceedings.

8.6   In *R.* v. *Inland Revenue Commissioners, ex p. Taylor,*[17] another difference emerged. The applicant sought discovery of reports referred to in an affidavit, on the grounds that they might demonstrate bad faith by the decision-maker, who had claimed to be relying on the reports. In civil proceedings, any documents referred to in affidavits and pleadings may normally be inspected.[18] However, because of the supervisory nature of judicial review, normally not all aspects of the decision will be relevant to the proceedings and it may therefore be more difficult to show that the production of a document is necessary for disposing fairly of the matter before the court. In *ex p. Taylor*, the court held that what was in issue in the review proceedings was the decision making process, not the contents of the documents considered, or the state of mind of the decision maker.

8.7   The court's approach to discovery is also affected by the greater likelihood, in public law proceedings, that the evidence as to which discovery is sought raises issues of public interest immunity,[19] or confidentiality.[20] The issue of public

---

[15]   *Ibid.*, p.635H.

[16]   *R.* v. *Secretary of State for the Home Department, ex p. B.H.* [1990] C.O.D. 445; *R.* v. *Secretary of State for the Environment, ex p. Islington L.B.C., The Independent*, 6 September 1991.

[17]   [1989] 1 All E.R. 906 (C.A.).

[18]   R.S.C., O. 24, r. 10(1).

[19]   *Air Canada* v. *Secretary of State for Trade* [1983] 2 A.C. 394.

interest immunity has led the courts to consider more closely the purpose of discovery in public law proceedings. In *Air Canada*, it was held that there must be a likelihood, based on some concrete grounds, for belief that discovery would support the party's case, and that discovery was necessary for the fair disposal of the issue.[21] Lord Scarman was in a minority in considering that the documents were necessary for fairly disposing of the cause if they gave substantial assistance to the court in determining the facts. Whereas he regarded the role of discovery as being not adversarial, but aimed at discovering the truth, the majority linked it to the fair determination of the issues as asserted by the parties.

8.8   In some cases, the absence of discovery (and other interlocutory process) may be overcome by conversion to writ procedure. This may help where either a declaration, or injunction or damages are being sought, but not a prerogative remedy. It would appear therefore, that there will continue to be proceedings in which prerogative remedies are sought, involving difficult factual issues for which, despite the availability of discovery, the courts are aware that the summary nature of judicial review procedure cannot be said to be just and convenient.

Options

8.9   It has been suggested that the provisions of R.S.C. Order 24 should apply to Crown proceedings (except to the extent that the documents lodged with the application or the respondent's affidavit make this unnecessary).[22] As there is no automatic discovery against the Crown, this might not avoid the court giving express consideration to cases where the Crown is the respondent, but might be of assistance in other cases.

8.10   On the other hand, it has also been put to us that discovery should be rarely granted, as the burden, cost and delay occasioned by discovery is very significant, both to the respondent body and to the success of the procedure in moving swiftly to determine the main issues which are not primarily factual issues.[23] In the case of the Crown discovery in itself is not a simple matter, given the indivisiblity of the Crown in all its emanations and the need to consider public interest immunity claims where appropriate. These considerations would argue in favour of maintaining a strict (or even stricter) approach to applications for discovery,

---

[20]   *Science Research Council* v. *Nassé* [1980] A.C. 1028.

[21]   [1983] 2 A.C. 394, Lord Fraser of Tullybelton, 435F-G; Lord Wilberforce, 438-439.

[22]   Administrative Law Bar Association submission.

[23]   Treasury Solicitor's Working Party.

perhaps that discovery should never be ordered unless there is a patent inconsistency on the affidavits and the record.[24]

8.11　　There appears to be disquiet that discovery is in practice being operated in a more restrictive way than would generally apply in civil proceedings. Some are unhappy that the applicant has to show an arguable case on the particular issue on which he seeks discovery and satisfy the court that the factual dispute is one for which discovery is necessary. Conscious deliberation of each application for discovery and the potential relevance of public interest immunity, are said to have made the courts and respondent bodies excessively cautious. On the other hand, while it is generally acknowledged that the principle that should be applied by the court is the ordinary principle applicable to discovery in civil proceedings, namely that production of a document should only be ordered if it is necessary for disposing fairly of the matter, it has been suggested to us that the nature of judicial review proceedings means that often there will be no case for discovery. This is because, in judicial review proceedings normally not all aspects of the relevant administrative decision will be in issue. For this reason, it is suggested that it would be reasonable to require the party seeking discovery to take the initiative, whether by making a specific application for discovery or otherwise. We invite views on the question whether there should be a more liberal regime for discovery in judicial review proceedings and if so, on what principles should it be based and how the particular burdens faced by the Crown might be met.

8.12　　There is a danger that if the present more restrictive regime is not relaxed, it will eventually be said that the reforms to Order 53 have not remedied the defects in interlocutory process claimed in *O'Reilly* and courts may be forced to re-open the alternative route of civil proceedings for declarations and injunctions. It may thus be counter-productive for courts to emphasise the distinct nature of judicial review proceedings in the context of applications for discovery and other related interlocutory process.

---

[24]　　As for example in *R. v. Secretary of State for the Home Department, ex p. B.H.* [1990] C.O.D. 445.

Background

9.1   The Commission's recommendations in 1976 led to a simplification of the requirements of standing, or *locus standi,* in the context of judicial review proceedings. The test now applicable, as provided by section 31(3) of the Supreme Court Act 1981, which only refers to the leave stage, is that the court must be of the opinion that the applicant has a sufficient interest in the matter to which the application relates. The new provision was considered by the House of Lords in the *National Federation of Self-Employed case*[1], which has been said to "crystallise the elements of a generous and public-oriented doctrine of standing which had previously been sporadic and uncoordinated."[2]

9.2   Although it is not altogether clear whether section 31(3) introduced a single test as to standing for all the remedies available by way of judicial review, procedural and technical differences have been removed. Attention now focuses on the statutory context and the nature of the applicant's interest in the case, rather than the remedy sought.[3]

9.3   The fluid nature of the requirement of sufficiency means that it is uncertain what precisely is required. Very broadly speaking, there are three possible approaches: to accord standing only where rights are affected; to accord it where, although the applicant's rights are not affected, she or he has in fact been adversely affected; and to accord it to all but the officious intermeddler, the "citizen action" approach. The predominant trend in the case law since the reform reflects a liberal approach which had long been a feature of relief by way of certiorari and prohibition, going beyond the protection of rights and "injury in fact" but with uneasiness about the treatment of decisions that affect the public in general, or a wide section of it. This contrasts with the position under Article 173 of the E.E.C. Treaty with regard to challenges to decisions of Community institutions. This only permits the institution of proceedings against Community institutions, by individuals as opposed to member States, where the individual is a person to whom a decision is addressed, or who is directly and individually concerned by a decision addressed to another.

---

[1]   [1982] A.C. 617.

[2]   H.W.R.Wade, *Administrative Law* (6th ed., 1988), p. 701.

[3]   *R.* v. *Inland Revenue Commissioners, ex. p. National Federation of Self-Employed and Small Businesses Ltd.* [1982] A.C. 617, 631C-F, 638, 645H-646D, 653F-G, 657-658; *R.* v. *Felixstowe JJ., ex p. Leigh* [1987] Q.B. 582.

Issues

9.4   Ultimately the options for reform depend on the view taken of the desirability of public interest challenges by individuals or groups. However, this section will first consider the basic rule, the position of those who are personally adversely affected, the role of the statutory context and the relevance of the seriousness of the illegality. These provide the necessary background to consideration of public interest challenges.

9.5   *At what stage or stages ought standing to be considered by the court?*   At the ex parte leave stage standing operates only to weed out hopeless applications by busy-bodies and mischief makers. The *National Federation of Self-Employed* case makes it clear that it is also relevant at the substantive hearing. The House of Lords held that sufficiency of interest depended on consideration of the full legal and factual context, i.e. the nature of the power or duty involved and the illegality alleged. Standing should not be considered separately from the substance or merits of the application, for instance as a preliminary issue.[4]

9.6   What was envisaged was a two-stage test of standing. It has, however, been suggested[5] that the practical effect of linking standing to the factual and legal context is to virtually eliminate from the full hearing a distinct test of standing, in the sense of a test of entitlement to raise and argue the issue because of a sufficient connection with it. If this is correct, the only true test of standing is the one applied at the leave stage. In *R. v. Secretary of State for Transport, ex p. Presvac Engineering Ltd.*, the Court of Appeal suggested that the test as to standing used at the full hearing really formed part of the exercise of the court's discretion whether to grant relief.[6] However, while standing is often not considered separately at the full hearing, it sometimes is[7] and the Court of Appeal has stated

---

[4]   Cf. *Finlay* v. *Canada (Minister of Finance)* [1986] 2 S.C.R. 607, 616-7 (Supreme Court of Canada).

[5]   H.W.R.Wade, *Administrative Law* (6th ed., 1988), p.703.

[6]   (1992) 4 Admin. L.R. 121. See also *R.* v. *Monopolies and Mergers Commission, ex p. Argyll Group Plc.* [1986] 1 W.L.R. 763, 774, where, Sir John Donaldson M.R.'s approach, although referring to a two-stage test, was similar. See also *Barrs* v. *Bethell* [1982] Ch. 294, 313 (leave requirement a filter justifying a less restrictive approach to standing).

[7]   e.g. *R.* v. *Secretary of State for the Environment, ex p. Rose Theatre Trust Co.* [1990] 1 Q.B. 504; *R* v. *Legal Aid Board, ex p. Bateman* [1992] 3 All E.R. 490 (C.A.). In neither case did the court consider that there was a good case on the merits for the relief sought.

56

that it is an issue that goes to the jurisdiction of the court.[8] The question is whether this should continue to be the case.

9.7   *Should there be separate and more certain treatment of those who are personally adversely affected?* Those whose private rights are infringed, who suffer special damage, over and above that suffered by the public at large, from the administrative action, or who have a financial stake in the outcome, will usually[9] have standing. For instance, the interest of competitors, challenging decisions concerning their commercial rivals, has sufficed, particularly where the issue raised is of discriminatory treatment.[10] However, such an interest is not necessary and the interest of those who are in fact adversely affected by a decision has also been recognised.[11] There are other situations where the impact of a decision on an individual is not substantial, or no more substantial than it is on other citizens but standing has been accorded. In such cases it is the nature of the individual's interest in the matter, or the public interest, rather than the fact that she or he has been affected, that is important.[12] The most notable example is the recognition that the interest of ratepayers may suffice even where the alleged breach of duty has no demonstrable effect on them.[13] Such cases, which often affect the public in general or a wide section of it, have tended to be more problematic.

9.8   Difficulties may also arise in cases where the statutory power or duty concerns, or is owed to an individual, or to a narrow range of individuals. In such cases an application by a person outside the designated category may fail for want of standing even where she or he is affected. Thus it is possible that only a person who has been dismissed, or has had her or his licence revoked, will have sufficient

---

[8]   *R. v. Secretary of State for Social Services, ex p. Child Poverty Action Group* [1990] 2 Q.B. 540, 556E.

[9]   But not always: *R. v. Commissioners of Customs and Excise, ex p. Cook* [1970] 1 W.L.R. 450; *R. v. Shemilt (A Taxing Officer), ex p. Buckley* [1988/89] C.O.D. 40.

[10]   *R. v. Thames Magistrates' Court, ex p. Greenbaum* (1957) 55 L.G.R. 129 (grant of market pitch); *R. v. Attorney-General, ex p. I.C.I. Plc.* [1987] 1 C.M.L.R. 588 (taxpayer's challenge to method used to value rival's profits).

[11]   *R. v. Secretary of State for the Environment, ex p. Ward* [1984] 1 W.L.R. 834; *Covent Garden Community Association v. G.L.C.* [1981] J.P.L. 183.

[12]   *R. v. H.M. Treasury, ex p. Smedley* [1985] Q.B. 657 (taxpayer's challenge to Government undertaking to pay contribution to European Community).

[13]   *Arsenal F.C. v. Ende* [1979] A.C. 1 ("person aggrieved" under statutory remedy).

interest to challenge the decision.[14] The position of an applicant who is not affected by a decision which has not been challenged by the person affected is even weaker.[15]

9.9   It may now be appropriate to treat cases in which the applicant has been personally adversely affected separately. For instance, following Lord Woolf's suggestion for a two-track approach,[16] the discretionary element in the way the rules operate could be reduced in this category of case by providing that those adversely affected should have standing, save in defined circumstances, such as those considered in paragraph 9.8 above. This approach has similarities to the distinction, made in the context of certiorari, between an application by a person aggrieved where the remedy lies *ex debito justitiae*, and an application by a "stranger" where the remedy is purely discretionary.[17] However, it differs in one important respect since the category of "person aggrieved" has included those, like ratepayers, who may not have been personally affected by the decision,[18] and may include any person who has a genuine grievance of whatever kind.[19]

9.10   *The role of the statutory context.* In the *National Federation of Self-Employed* case Lord Fraser said that the correct approach is "to look at the statute ... and to see whether it gives any express or implied right to persons in the position of the applicant to complain of the alleged unlawful act or omission."[20] Although this was said in the context of an alleged breach of statutory duty, it is equally applicable to statutory discretionary powers.[21]

---

[14]   *Durayappah* v. *Fernando* [1967] 2 A.C. 337 (as explained in *Hoffmann-La Roche & Co. A.G.* v. *Secretary of State for Trade and Industry* [1975] A.C. 295). See also *R.* v. *LAUTRO, ex p. Ross* (1991) 141 N.L.J. 1001 (Div. Ct.); [1992] 3 W.L.R. 549 (C.A.).

[15]   *R.* v. *Legal Aid Board, ex p. Bateman* [1992] 3 All E.R. 490.

[16]   "A Possible Programme for Reform", [1992] P.L. 221, 232-233.

[17]   *R.* v. *Thames Magistrates' Court, ex p. Greenbaum* (1957) 55 L.G.R. 129.

[18]   *R.* v. *Paddington Valuation Officer, ex p. Peachey Property Corpn. Ltd.* [1966] 1 Q.B. 380, 401.

[19]   See H.W.R.Wade, *Administrative Law* (6th ed., 1988), p. 746; JUSTICE-All Souls Report, *op. cit.*, p. 199, para. 8.51.

[20]   [1982] A.C. 617, 646C-D.

[21]   *R.* v. *Secretary of State for the Environment, ex p. Rose Theatre Trust Co.* [1990] 1 Q.B. 504, 507, 520-1.

9.11   However, while statutes may explicitly address the question of standing,[22] they often do not. In such cases the courts will take into account the nature of the power and whether it concerns and affects individuals, a section of the public or the public in general. The process is one of implication and the outcome may depend on the basic approach taken to access to the courts, on which there is a range of views. At one end there are those who do not see it as the function of the courts to be there for every individual who is interested in having the legality of all types of administrative action, including that affecting the public in general, litigated.[23] On this approach the function of the court is primarily to protect the personal interests of litigants. At the other there are those who believe it to be the function of the court to facilitate the hearing of such allegations by a so-called "citizen's action" or *actio popularis* so that, where they are made out, the rule of law can be vindicated.[24]

9.12   One solution, where the statute proves inconclusive, is the adoption of a presumption reflecting the desired starting point.[25] Thus, it has been suggested that "a citizen should be entitled at the discretion of the court to bring any action alleging invalid public activity, except where it can be shown from a consideration of the statutory framework that the range of persons with standing was intended to be narrower than this".[26] This virtually amounts to a "citizen action" and it might be thought to reflect the way the bulk of the case law has developed. However, as we shall see,[27] one recent decision indicates a more restrictive approach at any rate for decisions affecting the public in general. On this approach a different presumption would be appropriate, and in any event the variety of statutory contexts may well make a single presumption inappropriate.

9.13   *The relevance of the seriousness of the illegality alleged.* Dicta in the *National Federation of Self-Employed* case indicate that standing depends to some extent on

---

22   See for example, those set out at Annex 3, and paras. 19.9-19.12 below (relating to "person aggrieved").

23   *R. v. Secretary of State for the Environment, ex p. Rose Theatre Trust Co.* [1990] 1 Q.B. 504, 522C (Schiemann J.). See also Sir Konrad Schiemann, "Locus Standi", [1990] P.L. 342.

24   *National Federation of Self-Employed* case [1982] A.C. 617, 644, 654 (Lord Diplock and Lord Scarman).

25   See generally The Interpretation of Statutes (1969), Law Com. No. 21; Scot. Law Com. No. 11; paras. 34-39, especially para. 38 (determining whether civil liability arises from breach of statutory duty).

26   P.P.Craig, *Administrative Law* (2nd ed., 1989), p. 379.

27   See paras. 9.17-9.18 below.

this, with greater willingness to regard an interest as "sufficient", where grave, or widespread illegality is alleged.[28] The JUSTICE-All Souls Report said that this seemed fundamentally unsound since, subject to a *de minimis* principle, the courts ought to be able to act when a breach of the law by a public authority is drawn to their attention.[29] Quite apart from issues of principle, the more closely the question of the nature of the illegality is tied to the facts of the case, the more difficult it becomes to predict the degree of interest that will be required.

9.14   *Group challenges.*   The cases on the standing of representative groups to bring applications for judicial review focus on the sufficiency of interest by reference to the connection between the body and the matter in dispute. Thus, the National Union of Mineworkers and the Royal College of Nursing have been held to have standing to challenge decisions that affected their members.[30] As the groups in substance consisted of persons who were in fact affected by the decisions, we believe that this type of case should, in principle, pose no difficulties. It is relevant to note that individuals who are accorded standing are free to put their arguments on a much wider footing than their own particular interest might otherwise require. In this way both the public interest and individual interests in the challenged situation may be equally advanced. However, a clearer and less discretionary approach to standing, in cases where individuals or a distinct group have been adversely affected, may also be of assistance in this context.

9.15   Different issues are raised where a pressure group seeks to challenge a decision which concerns but does not directly affect its members. Such challenges have been allowed, where the group has been given statutory functions in relation to the category of decision,[31] or where the group is considered to be appropriate (perhaps because of its expertise) to represent the interests of those affected. For instance, the Child Poverty Action Group has been accorded standing to challenge decisions concerning social security which affected claimants.[32] This is in line

---

28   [1982] A.C. 617, 633, 647B, 654, 662.

29   *Op. cit.*, p. 196, para. 8.45.

30   *R.* v. *Chief Adjudication Officer, ex p. Bland, The Times,* 6 February 1985 (reduction of benefits to striking miners; cf. the T.U.C. whose connection was insufficient); *Royal College of Nursing of the U.K.* v. *D.H.S.S.* [1981] 1 All E.R. 545, 551b-h (Woolf J.), [1981] A.C. 800 (advice that it was lawful for nurses to carry out abortion where prescribed by a doctor who remained in charge).

31   *R.* v. *Secretary of State for Employment, ex p. Equal Opportunities Commission* [1992] 1 All E.R. 545 (Div. Ct.); *The Independent,* 10 November 1992 (C.A.).

32   *R.* v. *Secretary of State for Social Services, ex p. G.L.C., The Times,* 16 August 1984, (in the C.A. the point was left open, *The Times,* 8 August 1985); *R.* v. *Secretary of State for Social Services, ex p. Child Poverty Action Group* (1988)

with decisions in which individuals with a reasonable concern have been accorded standing, irrespective of whether they are affected in a way distinct from the general public,[33] although a recent decision,[34] considered below, calls into question the ability of pressure groups to institute judicial review proceedings. As such challenges whether by individuals or groups are really public interest challenges[35] they are considered below.

9.16   *Public Interest Challenges.*   Broadly speaking these fall into one of two categories. The first, exemplified by the cases considered in paragraph 9.15, is where, although the applicant is not affected in a different way from the general public, someone is. The second is where the decision concerns the public in general or a wide section of it. The fact that section 31(3) concentrates attention on the applicant's link with the subject matter of the case means that courts tend to focus on the fact that the challenger belongs to a particular category, such as ratepayer, resident, licence holder, journalist. This may deflect attention from important public interest aspects of a case and from the policy factors which should be taken into account, in deciding whether such an applicant is entitled to raise and argue the issue. It also means that the only clear example of a non-statutory pure public interest challenge in English law occurs where the Attorney-General brings an action, or is willing to act on "the relation" of a private individual who is liable for costs. However, such relator actions have been criticised as one sided[36] (since they are apparently not in practice available in proceedings against a Minister or the Government) and, in terms of judicial control of administrative action, inappropriate in principle, since the decision to permit proceedings is made by a minister and not, as under Order 53, by a judge, and is not even judicially reviewable.[37]   In the absence of acceptance by English law of the "citizen's action", successful public interest challenges are, moreover, difficult to explain in a wholly principled way and appear highly discretionary.

[1990] 2 Q.B. 540.

33   See the cases cited at para. 9.7 above. See also *R. v. G.L.C., ex p. Blackburn* [1976] 1 W.L.R. 550.

34   *R. v. Secretary of State for the Environment, ex p. Rose Theatre Trust Co.* [1990] 1 Q.B. 504.

35   *R. v. Felixstowe JJ., ex p. Leigh* [1987] Q.B. 582, 598.

36   H.W.R.Wade, *Administrative Law* (6th ed., 1988), p.605; JUSTICE-All Souls Report, *op. cit.*, pp. 186-190, paras. 8.22-8.32.

37   *Gouriet* v. *Union of Post Office Workers* [1978] A.C. 435.

9.17   Public interest challenges may require reassessment in the light of *R.* v. *Secretary of State for the Environment, ex p. Rose Theatre Trust Co..*[38] This case, which concerned challenge by a trust, which included *inter alios* acknowledged archaeological experts and local residents, of a decision not to schedule a site as a monument of national importance, calls into question the ability of pressure groups to institute judicial review proceedings. It was stated that the fact that a group joins together and asserts an interest does not create an interest if the individuals did not have one. The case also raises doubts about whether, in the absence of a positive indication in the relevant statute, anyone will have standing to challenge a general decision. The decision in question was said to be "one of those governmental decisions in respect of which the ordinary citizen does not have a sufficient interest to entitle him *to obtain leave* to move for judicial review" even though this may well leave an unlawful act by a Minister unrebuked.[39]

9.18   Although the decision may be explained by the particular statutory context and the statutory position of English Heritage,[40] the dicta suggest that it may have been influenced by a particular view of the function of the court.[41] However, at a time of increased pressure on the Crown Office list and delays it may also reflect a wider concern to ensure that scarce judicial resources are allocated optimally.

Options for reform

9.19   There are a number of different ways in which reform might be approached on which we invite views. It is first necessary to form a view about two basic questions:

(a) Is it correct in principle to allow public interest challenges to administrative decisions, whether by individuals or by groups?

(b) Should the principles upon which the court will grant or refuse standing be formulated in a less fluid way than the present provisions?

---

[38]   [1990] 1 Q.B. 504, noted by P.Cane, "Statutes, Standing and Representation", [1990] P.L. 307.

[39]   *R.* v. *Secretary of State for Environment, ex p. Rose Theatre Trust Co.* [1990] 1 Q.B. 504, 521G (emphasis added).

[40]   A body with a statutory duty *inter alia* to secure the preservation of ancient monuments and historic buildings and which the Minister was required to consult before deciding to schedule a site.

[41]   See para. 9.11 above.

9.20   A decision not to entertain public interest challenges would constitute a fundamental change to the law. In view of the unsatisfactory aspects of the Attorney-General's relator action, it would be important to develop an alternative if reform of the test of standing precluded or imposed further limits on group and public interest challenges. One possibility would be to introduce a central figure with responsibility for bringing all public interest challenges: as in Lord Woolf's proposal for a Director of Civil Proceedings.[42]

9.21   If group challenges and public interest challenges are considered desirable in certain circumstances, the issues raised above could be addressed in a number of ways.

(a) The provisions as to standing in the Supreme Court Act and Order 53 could expressly refer to the public interest as well as to the applicant's link with the subject matter of the case, as recommended by the JUSTICE-All Souls Report.

(b) The present uncertainties could be addressed by referring in legislation or rules to factors, other than the applicant's link with the subject-matter, to be taken into account in determining whether an application is justifiable in the public interest. A number of factors have been suggested.[43] These include: the importance of the legal point, the chances of the issue being raised in any other proceeding, the allocation of scarce judicial resources, and the concern that in the determination of issues the courts should have the benefit of the conflicting points of view of those most directly affected by them. We invite comment on the appropriateness and relative importance of these, or any other, factors.

9.22   As regards group challenges, we have referred to statutory functions and appropriateness because of expertise as two of the factors that may be relevant[44] and invite views as to whether there are any other factors which the court should take into account in deciding whether a particular group has standing.

9.23   Whatever approach is taken on public interest challenges, the following questions arise:

(a) Should those adversely affected by a decision or a regulation and groups of such persons be subject to a separate and less discretionary requirement of standing which would clarify their entitlement to be heard, save in specified circumstances?

---

[42]   *Hamlyn Lectures*, pp. 109-113.

[43]   By the JUSTICE-All Souls Report, *op. cit.*, pp. 203-204, para. 8.61, p.208 and by Sir Harry Woolf, "A Possible Programme for Reform", [1992] P.L. 221, at 233.

[44]   Para. 9.15 above.

(b) Would it be useful, as discussed in paragraph 9.12, to have a presumption as a long stop where an examination of the statute proves inconclusive. If so, should it apply in all cases or only in the case of decisions affecting a section of the public or the public in general?

9.24   The way in which standing is considered at the leave stage might also be reformed. If a major purpose of leave is to save respondents from incurring the direct and indirect costs of litigation, it may be appropriate for standing to be more fully considered at the leave stage.[45] If there are factors in the present mechanism for leave precluding the court from properly considering the issue of standing, that is a matter which ought to be addressed by remedying the leave procedure.

9.25   If, however, standing is considered in depth at the leave stage, should it be considered at the stage of the substantive application, and, if so, how should it be treated? It seems *prima facie* wasteful both of judicial time and in costs to determine the same issue twice in the same proceedings.

Provisional View

9.26   It is in our view appropriate that a broad test of standing to raise an issue of public law should be maintained. We suggest that this should be made more explicit in legislation or rules along the lines suggested in paragraph 9.21. Such a test recognises the appropriateness, in certain circumstances, of public interest challenges to regulations and decisions including decisions affecting the public in general. We invite views as to the factors which should be taken into account by the court in considering whether an applicant satisfies the test. We also invite views as to the relative importance of the factors indicative of sufficient interest.

9.27   We are concerned that the implication in the *Rose Theatre* case is that, in the absence of positive indications in the relevant statute, neither an ordinary citizen nor a well qualified expert may have standing to challenge an otherwise justiciable decision which affects the public in general. We disagree with the suggestion that the test of standing is aimed at reducing uncertainty and chaos and the need to discourage over-cautious decision-making.[46] Uncertainty and chaos are more appropriately addressed by other mechanisms, particularly time limits. The danger of provoking over-cautious decision-making is a factor to be considered when deciding whether a decision is invalid or reviewable, not when deciding who has standing to challenge it. Also, while the *nature* of the power or duty allegedly

---

[45]   Sir Konrad Schiemann, "Locus Standi", [1990] P.L. 342, 351.

[46]   [1990] 1 Q.B. 504, 519, 521.

breached is relevant to the question of standing, the seriousness or widespread nature of the illegality should not be relevant.

9.28   We invite comments on whether it should be possible to apply for judicial review raising a public interest challenge in the two categories of situation referred to above in para 9.16, i.e. either where an individual has been specially affected but the application is brought by another person or group, or where no individual has been specially affected but the decision affects the public in general. If so, we invite views as to the circumstances in which such challenges ought to be permitted, how standing should be tested, and whether such challenges should be within the framework of Order 53, or in some other way, such as by a central figure with responsibility for bringing all public interest challenges, such as a Director of Civil Proceedings,[47] or by relator action or otherwise.

---

[47]   See para. 9.20 above.

10.1   Following the Commission's 1976 recommendations, claims for damages could be joined with applications for judicial review. The purpose was to avoid multiplicity of proceedings by bringing together claims arising out of the same events. However, Order 53, unlike the equivalent provision in Scotland,[1] makes no provision for joinder of restitutionary claims.[2] The development of the exclusivity principle in *O'Reilly* v. *Mackman*, discussed in section 3 above and the recent proceedings between the *Woolwich Equitable Building Society* and the *Inland Revenue* suggest that there is a gap which should be closed.

10.2   The *Woolwich* case established that money paid by a citizen to a public authority in the form of taxes or other levies paid pursuant to an ultra vires demand by the authority is prima facie recoverable by the citizen as of right.[3] In that case the unlawfulness of the demand had in fact been established in judicial review proceedings before the action for restitution was finally decided.[4] Although it is not altogether clear whether judicial review proceedings are a necessary preliminary to the restitutionary action the fact that there is a right to restitution suggests that they should not be.[5]

Provisional View

10.3   Whether or not it is a prerequisite to the restitutionary claim that the unlawfulness of the demand be established in judicial review proceedings, on the reasoning used by the Commission in 1976, it would appear that there are good reasons for allowing restitutionary claims to be joined with applications for judicial review. We would welcome views on this issue.

---

[1]   Act of Sederunt (Rules of Court Amendment No. 2)(Judicial Review) 1985, S.I. 1985, No. 500.

[2]   See *Wandsworth L.B.C.* v. *Winder* [1985] A.C. 461, 480E-D, 484D (per Robert Goff and Parker L.JJ.).

[3]   *Woolwich Equitable Building Society* v. *Inland Revenue Commissioners* [1992] 3 W.L.R. 366, 396C-D, 415E-F, 421G-H (H.L.).

[4]   *R.* v. *Inland Revenue Commissioners, ex p. Woolwich Equitable Building Society* [1990] 1 W.L.R. 1400 (H.L.).

[5]   See paras. 3.2-3.8 and 3.11-3.12 above; Restitution of Payments Made Under a Mistake of Law (1991), Law Com. C.P. No. 120, para. 3.47; *Woolwich Equitable Building Society* v. *I.R.C.* [1991] 3 W.L.R. 790, 797, 817-818, 835, 852, (C.A.); [1992] 3 W.L.R. 366, 388F, 393A-F, 417G-H (Lord Goff and Lord Slynn). Cf. *Colne Valley Water Co.* v. *National Rivers Authority* (Unreported) 20 December 1990, (Millett J.).

Background

11.1   Awards of costs (i.e. inter partes costs governed by R.S.C., Order 62) are in the court's discretion but they generally follow the event, so that the party who wins is entitled to costs from the other side. This approach applies generally, both in civil proceedings and Crown side proceedings. We consider here the application of the current provisions for costs in the context of public law litigation, the extent of the courts' power to award costs in judicial review proceedings and the issues which are currently problematical in this area.

11.2   Costs are rarely awarded in relation to the ex parte leave stage unless some other claim is joined with the leave application, such as for ex parte injunctive relief.[1] It has been held,[2] indeed, that the power of the court to order payment of costs of judicial review proceedings under, section 51 of the Supreme Court Act 1981,[3] does not arise until leave to move for judicial review has been granted.

11.3   The ex parte nature of the leave stage, even if conducted on the papers and without an oral hearing, may generate significant costs if the applicant is legally represented. There is some evidence that the costs referable to obtaining counsel's opinion as to merits, prior to initiating applications for leave and seeking legal aid, may amount to £1000.[4] Such figures are in stark contrast to Lord Woolf's extra-judicial comment that the opinion of a High Court judge could be obtained for only £10 by a hypothetical litigant in person.[5] In considering the litigant's access to judicial review, it is surely important that courts and litigants have some realistic knowledge of the measure of costs to which parties are exposed. We hope that the Public Law Project may be able to contribute some information on this issue, but it is a matter on which we would also welcome information from practitioners.

---

[1]   As in *R.* v. *Committee of Advertising Practice, ex p. Bradford Exchange* [1991] C.O.D. 43.

[2]   *R.* v. *Test Valley Borough Council, ex p. Goodman* [1992] C.O.D. 101.

[3]   Now as substituted by s.4 of the Courts and Legal Services Act 1990.

[4]   Lee Bridges, paper delivered to seminar on Judicial Review for Legal Aid Practitioners, held at University College London, June 1992.

[5]   "Public Law - Private Law: Why the Divide? A Personal View", [1986] P.L. 220, 230.

11.4   We have been told[6] that the ex parte nature of leave (i.e. the lack of opportunity for respondents to make representations) can have the effect that cases which ought to have been refused leave are granted leave and their continuation leads to respondents incurring costs which would not have arisen if the application for leave had been inter partes. On the other hand we have been told that a "cottage industry" is developing in relation to counsel being instructed to attend and oppose ex parte applications, in this way incurring costs.[7]

11.5   Where the proceedings are discontinued after leave has been granted, the respondent will only recover its costs if the discontinuance could safely be equated with defeat or an acknowledgement of likely defeat. Where the discontinuance follows some step by the respondent or a third party which renders the proceedings academic, the parties will bear their own costs.[8] If, however, it is clear that the respondent has acted to preempt failure in the proceedings, it may be just that he or she should pay the applicant's costs.

11.6   Where a case progresses to the main hearing, the same general approach to costs applies as in civil proceedings or appeals. It is still rare for costs to be ordered against lower tribunals such as magistrates and coroners, even if the applicant succeeds. There is a general tendency (explicitly adopted in relation to magistrates) for the decision maker not to appear unless its character or bona fides is questioned or unless specifically invited.

11.7   Where there are two or more applicants or respondents, the court will generally seek to avoid duplication of costs by awarding only one set of costs, unless the case raises complex issues. In *Bolton Borough Council* v. *Secretary of State for the Environment and the British Coal Corporation*,[9] the court noted the growing willingness of courts to recognise the vested interest which the owner of land had concerning the validity of a grant of planning permission, sufficient to justify allowing the owner the separate costs of defending his or her rights in court.

Issues

11.8   In our discussion of the leave stage,[10] we have suggested some developments in the power to use paper representations prior to the leave hearing to obtain the

---

[6]   By the Society of Local Authority Chief Executives.

[7]   Administrative Law Bar Association submission.

[8]   *R.* v. *Liverpool City Council, ex p. Newman, The Times*, 3 November 1992.

[9]   [1989] C.O.D. 352.

[10]   See section 5.

respondent's comments without generating inordinate costs. The need to minimise costs mirrors the need for speed, however, and there seems no virtue in promoting reforms which increase both cost and delay. We welcome views on the extent to which costs rules might be used to further the purpose of the leave stage whilst minimising the costs expended at that stage.

The principle of awarding costs to the successful party

11.9   Reference has been made above to the general rule that costs follow the event. The counter argument to awards of costs, particularly liability to pay the other side's costs, in proceedings brought in the public interest has been put to us.[11] It is suggested that where an application brought in good faith in the public interest is unsuccessful, the applicant should not be obliged to pay the other side's costs (though they might be left to pay their own costs).

11.10   Furthermore, it could be said that the usual principle of costs being awarded to the successful party is really designed for civil litigation concerning the vindication of private rights, not Crown side proceedings for public law supervision or even for criminal law proceedings. The applicant, by initiating the issue of Crown side proceedings is enabling the court to exercise its supervisory jurisdiction at the behest of the Crown. It is the Crown that has a major interest in the courts exercising proper supervisory control of decision-making bodies and this might properly be reflected in special rules as to costs.

Costs from Central Funds

11.11   A further contentious issue at present is the power of courts to awards costs from central funds in civil cases. Until recently it was thought that there was no power to award costs from central funds except where statute had specifically provided monies for that purpose. However, the Divisional Court and the Court of Appeal have held in three recent cases that there is no warrant for restricting the wide words of section 51 of the 1981 Act to prevent awards of costs from central funds when justice so demands.[12] The *Holden* case is currently under appeal to the House of Lords.

---

[11]   U.K. Environmental Law Association.

[12]   *Ex p. Central Television Plc.* [1991] 1 W.L.R. 4, (C.A.); *R. v. Bow Street Metropolitan Stipendiary Magistrate, ex parte Mirror Group Newspapers Ltd.; R. v. Same ex p. British Broadcasting Corporation* [1992] 1 W.L.R. 412; *Holden & Co. v. Crown Prosecution Service (No. 2)* [1992] 1 W.L.R. 407, (C.A.), (Div. Ct.).

11.12   To qualify for an order for costs under section 18(4) of the Legal Aid Act 1988,
         a respondent has to demonstrate that it will suffer severe financial hardship unless
         an order is made, and that it is just and equitable for the court to order such
         costs.[13] It has been suggested to us[14] that it is inequitable that non-legally aided
         respondents (particularly local authorities) should not be entitled to their reasonable
         legal costs of an unsuccessful application for judicial review. Whereas the severe
         financial hardship test provides relief in theory, the cases indicate that an order on
         these grounds will not be made in favour of an institution with adequate financial
         resources.[15]

11.13   We invite the views of consultees on the availability of legal aid for judicial
         review.[16] One issue is the manner in which the legal aid test relates to the
         appropriateness of the particular applicant to bring the application and to the issue
         of contribution from other potential beneficiaries. A second relates to the
         implications of the decision in *R.* v. *Legal Aid Board, ex p. Hughes*[17] concerning
         the merits tests that are applied by the court in granting leave and by the Legal Aid
         Board in granting assistance. The Court of Appeal held that the tests were
         essentially the same, and it may be questioned whether it is logical that the Legal
         Aid Board and the court may arrive at different conclusions on the same test.

Provisional View

11.14   Where leave has been granted on the footing that the application discloses arguable
         grounds that the court ought to exercise its prerogative jurisdiction, we consider
         that it may be appropriate to disapply the usual costs rules, on the footing that they
         are inappropriate to the nature of the jurisdiction. How this should be formulated
         and whether there should be conditions are matters on which we invite comments.

---

[13]   If the court is acting as an appellate court, rather than a court of first instance, only
        the "just and equitable" test applies: *R.* v. *London Borough of Greenwich, ex p.
        Lovelace and Fay, (No. 2)* (1992) 4 Admin. L.R. 406.

[14]   K. Pugsley, Director of Law and Administration of Dacorum Borough Council.

[15]   *Kelly* v. *London Transport Executive* [1982] 1 W.L.R. 1055.

[16]   As indicated in paragraph 1.3 above, the availability of legal aid for judicial review
        is also being examined by the Public Law Project and responses which take account
        of their preliminary report would be particularly helpful.

[17]   (1992) 142 N.L.J. 1304 (C.A.).

RENEWED APPLICATIONS AND APPEALS FROM REFUSAL OF SUBSTANTIVE APPLICATION FOR JUDICIAL REVIEW

Background

12.1 Different provisions apply to criminal causes and matters, and civil causes. For criminal causes, the decision of a Divisional Court may only be appealed to the House of Lords.[1] This requires leave and a certificate that a point of law of general public importance is involved which ought to be considered by the House of Lords. In civil causes, if leave to move has been granted and the substantive application heard, there is a right of appeal to the Court of Appeal. If the Court of Appeal makes the substantive order on the judicial review application,[2] there is an appeal, with leave, to the House of Lords.

12.2 In civil as in criminal proceedings the jurisdiction to grant prerogative remedies has been conferred on the High Court. The jurisdiction should accordingly be exercised by the designated body, i.e. in this case the High Court rather than the Court of Appeal or the House of Lords.

12.3 In judicial review appeals arising out of criminal causes the rules overtly direct the court to consider whether the case raises a point of law of general public importance, which fits well with the general public law purpose of the reviewing jurisdiction. By contrast, judicial review appeals arising out of civil causes are determined by the general rules for civil appeals and the classification of the order appealed from.

Renewal of Applications

12.4 In judicial review applications relating to criminal causes, a refusal of leave (or a grant on terms) made without a hearing can be renewed to the Divisional Court.[3]

12.5 In civil cases a refusal of leave may be renewed but not appealed.[4] Where the application for leave was made on the papers it may be renewed before either a single judge or, if the court so directs, a Divisional Court. An applicant is allowed only one hearing in the High Court so where the initial refusal of leave is from an

---

[1]   i.e. there is no appeal to the Court of Appeal.

[2]   As in the circumstances of a renewed application, mentioned below at para. 12.7.

[3]   R.S.C., O.53, rule 3(4)(a).

[4]   R.S.C., O.53, rule 3(4).

oral hearing the application can only then be renewed to the Court of Appeal.[5] Unlike civil proceedings, the renewal of an application before the Court of Appeal for leave to move for judicial review does not itself require leave from either the single judge or the Court of Appeal. The House of Lords has no jurisdiction to hear an appeal against the refusal of a renewed application for leave.[6]

12.6   The applicant's right of access without leave to the Court of Appeal was debated in the course of the Administration of Justice Bill in 1985. Clause 43 of that Bill sought to remove the right of appeal to the Court of Appeal. This proved contentious and was defeated in the House of Lords.[7] A revised clause sought to replace the right of appeal to the Court of Appeal with a requirement that the leave of the Court of Appeal should be obtained, combined with the possibility of a second oral hearing (as of right) before a Divisional Court containing one member of the Court of Appeal.[8] Neither proposal was accepted and the procedure as described above was left unchanged.

12.7   Where the Court of Appeal grants leave on a renewed application, the application is generally remitted to be heard by a single judge, but the Court of Appeal may, in exceptional circumstances, proceed to hear the substantive application, e.g. if an appeal to the Court of Appeal is inevitable because the judge finds herself or himself bound by a judgment of the Divisional Court.[9] Respondents may apply to have leave set aside.[10] It is unclear whether a challenge by the applicant to the order to have leave set aside in the Court of Appeal constitutes a renewed application for leave to move for judicial review or an application for leave to

---

[5]   R.S.C., O. 59, r. 14(3).

[6]   *Re Poh* [1983] 1 W.L.R. 2.

[7]   *Hansard* (H.L.), 5 February 1985, vol. 459, cols. 939-954.

[8]   *Hansard* (H.L.), 19 March 1985, vol. 461, cols. 443-464.

[9]   *Practice Direction (Judicial Review: Appeals),* 2 November 1982, [1982] 1 W.L.R. 1375. We have been told that this has actually occurred.

[10]   R.S.C., O. 32, r.6; and see *R.* v. *Secretary of State for the Home Department, ex p. Begum* [1990] C.O.D. 107 (C.A.).

appeal against the order.[11] The House of Lords has no jurisdiction to hear an appeal against the refusal of a renewed application for leave.[12]

Provisional Views

12.8   We tend to the view that any right of appeal from a decision of the High Court on judicial review ought to be cast by reference to the wider general importance of the disputed issue. We note Lord Donaldson's suggestion that a requirement of leave should be introduced for all appeals to the Court of Appeal, including, presumably, judicial review.[13]

12.9   We invite views on the present provisions for appeals and the need to align and clarify the provisions for appeals from substantive orders made on judicial review. The following alternatives are suggested, for comment.

(a)   In civil causes, restrict appeals to the Court of Appeal from the High Court by providing that they should be subject to leave, the primary ground for the grant of leave being that the appeal raises a point of law of general public importance, or

(b)   In civil causes, exclude appeals to the Court of Appeal or to the House of Lords, except where the High Court (or the Court of Appeal or House of Lords) certifies that a point of law of general public importance is involved.

(c)   In criminal causes, empower appeals to the Court of Appeal as an alternative to the House of Lords, where the High Court certifies that a point of general public importance is involved.

12.10   We appreciate the need for flexibility in the judicial arrangements for the initial consideration and renewal of applications for leave, whether before a single judge with or without a hearing, or a Divisional Court, but such arrangements ought to be justified on grounds of principle as well as convenience. We invite views on whether the present arrangements operate fairly, or require more explicit justification.

---

[11]   In *R. v. Secretary of State for the Home Department, ex p. Doorga* [1990] Imm. A.R. 98 (C.A.) the question was left open but different views have been expressed in two other C.A. decisions: *R. v. Secretary of State for the Home Department, ex p. Soon Ok Ryoo, The Independent*, 5 July 1991 and *R. v. Secretary of State for the Home Department, ex p. Al-Nafeesi* [1990] C.O.D. 262.

[12]   *Re Poh* [1983] 1 W.L.R. 2.

[13]   Lord Donaldson M.R. in *R. v. Foreign and Commonwealth Office, ex p. Kalibala, The Times*, 23 October 1991 and the Court of Appeal's Annual Report 1990-1991.

12.11   We also invite views as to whether the difficulties in distinguishing between renewals of leave and appeals arising out of the setting aside of leave ought to be resolved and if so, how.

13

POWER TO SUBSTITUTE ORDER FOR THAT OF THE IMPUGNED DECISION

13.1   Where the High Court considers that there are grounds for quashing the decision of a lower court, tribunal or authority, the High Court may, in addition to quashing the order, remit the matter to the lower court etc. with a direction to reconsider it and reach a decision in accordance with the findings of the Court.[1] The High Court does not have power to substitute its own order. It has been suggested to us that there might be situations in which it would be better if the High Court when quashing the order complained of, were able to substitute its own order for that of the lower court, tribunal or decision-maker. This might avoid further costs and inconvenience to the parties or the lower court or tribunal. The question is whether it is ever possible for a reviewing court properly to do this.

13.2   The policy relevant to the development of tribunals outside the court structure,[2] which applies equally to the inferior courts such as magistrates' courts and county courts and to other administrative decision makers, is that within the proper scope of their jurisdiction the lower court or tribunal etc. should be responsible for decision-making, developing the body of expertise relevant to its field of operation. Judicial review procedure exists to force inferior courts and tribunals, if necessary, to determine disputes and not to sidestep their responsibilities. The remedy of mandamus is also aimed at insisting that lower courts perform their proper role in decision making. The issue of substitution thus straddles considerations relevant to both the appellate and review roles of the High Court, and the hesitations that we have expressed in previous sections of this paper, as to the danger of confusion of these roles, apply *a fortiori* here.

13.3   Where a decision is judicially reviewed on the ground of breach of natural justice or abuse of discretion there will often be more than one permissible answer open to the lower court or administrative body. In such cases a power of substitution would be incompatible with the court's reviewing function. However, this may not be the case where the ground of review is error of law.[3] Where the grounds for

---

[1]   O. 53, r.9(4).

[2]   Discussed, for example, in the Report of the Franks Committee on Administrative Tribunals and Inquiries (1957), Cmnd. 218.

[3]   Although in theory situations in which there is only one possible inference from the primary facts are susceptible to the same argument (see the facts in *R.* v. *Rowe, ex p. Mainwaring* [1992] 1 W.L.R. 1059 (C.A.), a power of substitution could risk the court going beyond its reviewing function.

review are that there has been an error of law which, once corrected, necessarily leads to an obvious outcome, an order remitting the case to that court may now appear to be a remnant of an outmoded and unjustified insistence on procedural propriety.

13.4   We invite views as to whether there are any circumstances in which it might be appropriate to allow the High Court to substitute its order for that of the lower tribunal.

Background

14.1   The element of discretion lies at the heart of the remedies available by way of judicial review. The discretionary nature of remedies is common both to the prerogative remedies of certiorari, mandamus and prohibition, and to the equitable remedies of injunction and declaration which were, in 1977, added to the remedies available by way of judicial review. The discretionary element is also obvious at various stages in the procedure, and has been referred to earlier in our discussion of the leave requirement, delay, the grant of interim relief, and the question of standing. The factors taken into account by the courts in the exercise their discretion to grant or refuse relief when a ground for judicial review has been established include: waiver, bad faith, and ulterior motives, prematurity, absence of injustice or prejudice, impact on third parties and on the administration, the fact that the decision would have been the same irrespective of the error and the procedural nature of the error.[1]

Issues arising in relation to the discretionary nature of remedies

14.2   As the scope of judicially reviewable decisions has widened and public awareness of the potential availability of a remedy has increased, the differences between remedies available as of right, and those which are discretionary have been more in debate.[2] In recent years discussion of public law "rights" as a more substantive matter has prompted questions as to the nature of the courts' discretion. It has also provoked discussion as to whether the grounds being developed by the courts for granting or refusing to exercise their discretion when a ground for judicial review has been established are satisfactory and operate in a reasonably predictable way. "[P]rovided the discretion is strictly limited and the rules for its exercise clearly understood",[3] the mere fact that it exists in this context as it does in others, should not, in our view be a cause for concern.

14.3   A second issue arising in relation to the discretionary nature of remedies is the extent to which the merits of a case appear to influence a court's willingness to

---

[1]   H.W.R. Wade, *Administrative Law* (6th ed., 1988), pp. 709-719; C.Lewis, *Judicial Remedies in Public Law* (1992), pp. 283 ff.

[2]   Sir Thomas Bingham, "Should Public Law Remedies be Discretionary?", [1991] P.L. 64.

[3]   *Ibid.*, at 64 and 75.

exercise its discretion. The factor of merit is sometimes considered under the guise of the inevitability of the outcome,[4] or where there is an issue of natural justice and there are doubts as to the utility of the remedy.[5] Consideration of the merits may in some cases be inextricably linked with the supervisory and appellate elements of the High Court's jurisdiction over inferior courts. In other cases, it may be seen as part of the proper and necessary consideration to be given to the substance of the alleged unfairness. One particular criticism concerning the relevance of considering merit in judicial review, however, is that it contributes to the blurring of the distinction between appellate and review functions. We invite practitioners to comment on whether the need to anticipate an attack on the merits of an application in the context of the exercise of discretion has affected the conduct and length of proceedings.

14.4   A third area of debate concerns the discretionary denial of judicial review for reasons of public administration. We have discussed this issue in the context of time limits.[6] Lord Donaldson M.R. in *Ex parte Argyll Group Plc.*[7] drew attention to the need for decisiveness, speed and finality in decision making and the entitlement of the financial community to rely on the finality of the Monopolies Commission's announced decision.

14.5   A related issue arises from statements that in certain situations, although the grounds for review are established, the court will not in general grant a remedy except by way of declaratory relief on an historic footing.[8] The court will refuse to interfere with administrative action contemporaneously. The considerations taken into account by courts include the extent to which it is imperative that third parties be able to rely on a decision,[9] the fact that third parties who have relied on it would be unfairly prejudiced, and the danger of tactical applications for judicial

---

[4]   *R.* v. *Monopolies and Mergers Commission, ex p. Argyll Group Plc.* [1986] 1 W.L.R. 763.

[5]   *Glynn* v. *Keele University* [1971] 1 W.L.R. 487.

[6]   See section 4.

[7]   [1986] 1 W.L.R. 763.

[8]   *R.* v. *Secretary of State for Social Services, ex p. A.M.A.* [1986] 1 W.L.R. 1 (regulations concerning housing benefit); *R.* v. *Panel on Take-overs and Mergers, ex p. Datafin Plc.* [1987] Q.B. 815, 842; *R.* v. *Panel on Take-overs and Mergers, ex p. Guinness Plc.* [1990] 1 Q.B. 146 (urgent and financially sensitive decision making relied on by the market); *R.* v. *Dairy Produce Quota Tribunal, ex p. Caswell* [1989] 1 W.L.R. 1089, aff'd [1990] 2 A.C. 738.

[9]   *R.* v. *Panel on Take-overs and Mergers, ex p. Datafin Plc. and ex p. Guinness Plc.* ibid..

review.[10]   Although, many applicants are, in our view, unlikely to bring proceedings and expose themselves to the risk of costs where it is probable that a remedy will only be given on an historic basis, there may be situations in which such a remedy can be justified in principle and would be useful to certain types of applicant. Reliance on the invalidity of the impugned act would not be precluded in any subsequent disciplinary action[11] and in some cases relief which is in effect prospective[12] may be given. The court, while refusing relief in respect of the particular decision that is the subject of the application, deals with the general question of law that the case raises and provides guidance for the future. We invite consultees' views on these questions.

Alternative Remedies

14.6   There is also a particularly problematic area concerning the discretionary denial of remedies where an alternative remedy to judicial review is potentially available. Although on occasion and in certain contexts courts have indicated a preference for judicial review as opposed to a statutory remedy,[13] as a general principle, alternative remedies must be exhausted before resorting to judicial review.[14] This would generally be addressed at the leave stage, but might also be taken at the main hearing.[15]

14.7   Several different considerations are used by courts to justify this approach. First, where Parliament has determined that the best forum for challenging decisions is an appellate body, it is not for the courts to usurp the functions of the appellate body.[16] Second, the public interest is best served by a speedy judicial review procedure; given the constraints on judicial resources, this is thought to justify

---

[10]   *R.* v. *Panel on Take-overs and Mergers, ex p. Guinness Plc.*, [1990] 1 Q.B. 146.

[11]   *Ibid.*.

[12]   C. Lewis, "Retrospective and Prospective Rulings in Administrative Law", [1988] P.L. 78.

[13]   *Ellis & Sons Fourth Amalgamated Properties* v. *Southern Rent Assessment Panel* (1984) 270 E.G. 39; *Bone* v. *Mental Health Tribunal* [1985] 3 All E.R. 330. See also *R.* v. *Secretary of State for the Home Department, ex p. Malhi* [1991] 1 Q.B. 194, 207, 211 and paras. 18.10 and 19.21 below.

[14]   See *R.* v. *Epping and Harlow General Commissioners, ex p. Goldstraw* [1983] 3 All E.R. 257, 262j.

[15]   *R.* v. *Secretary of State for the Home Department, ex p. Swati* [1986] 1 W.L.R. 477.

[16]   See *R.* v. *Panel on Take-overs and Mergers, ex p. Guinness Plc.* [1990] 1 Q.B. 146, 177H.

limiting the number of cases in which leave to apply should be given.[17] Third, appeals address more fully the issues involved in a disputed decision, especially where facts are contested. Whilst judicial review may, in the case of certiorari, quash the particular decision, it rarely resolves the substantive merits.

14.8 In *R. v. Chief Constable of the Merseyside Police, ex p. Calveley*,[18] the Court of Appeal considered the requirement to exhaust alternative remedies unless there are exceptional circumstances as stated in *ex p. Goldstraw*. The Court stated that it was not to be regarded or construed as a statute. Where an appellate procedure itself contained elements of prejudice or possible breaches of natural justice, the court would exercise its discretion to grant judicial review. Other factors identified as relevant were: whether the alternative remedy would resolve the question at issue fully and directly, whether it would be quicker or slower than judicial review and whether the appeal body possessed special expertise.[19]

14.9 These factors point to the considerations which the court will apply in weighing the relative effectiveness and convenience of the alternative remedies, rather than identify what qualify as "exceptional circumstances". It has been argued that the "exceptional circumstances" principle acts as a rhetorical device.[20] It would appear in some cases to have been used to deter unmeritorious applicants from turning first to judicial review, whereas in more meritorious cases a more flexible approach has been applied.[21]

Criticisms of the requirement to exhaust alternative remedies

14.10 There are situations in which a right of appeal does not appear to extend to the heart of the issue which is challenged. In *Chief Adjudication Officer v. Foster*[22] it was held that the appellate tribunal did not have jurisdiction to determine the validity of the regulations which lay at the heart of the grounds of the appellant's appeal on a point of law. Similarly, the scope of a right of appeal may not

---

17   *Ibid.*, 177H-178A.

18   [1986] 1 Q.B. 424.

19   See *Ex parte Waldron* [1986] Q.B. 824, 852 G-H, (*per* Glidewell L.J.).

20   Sir Thomas Bingham, "Should Public Law Remedies be Discretionary?", [1991] P.L. 64, p. 72.

21   Contrast *R. v. Epping and Harlow General Commissioners, ex p. Goldstraw* [1983] 3 All E.R. 257 and *R. v. Commissioner for the Special Purposes of the Income Tax Acts, ex p. Napier* [1988] 3 All E.R. 166 with *Ex p. Waldron* [1986] Q.B. 824 and *R. v. Inspector of Taxes, ex p. Kissane* [1986] 2 All E.R. 37.

22   [1992] Q.B. 31 (C.A.). See para. 18.33 below.

empower the appellate body to overturn a decision for breach of natural justice, abuse of power or *Wednesbury* unreasonableness.[23] It has also been suggested that, where there is a right as a matter of law to have a decision quashed, it is pointless to require an applicant first to pursue an appeal on the merits.[24]

14.11   Where applicants use the appeal procedure, they may find that only the appeal decision and not the original decision will thereafter be deemed reviewable.[25] Where an appeal is a *de novo* hearing the courts are inclined to hold that the appeal is able to cure a flawed initial decision.[26] In this way, an appeal may obliterate the potentially reviewable issue in the original decision, leaving appellants with no apparent ground for review, and forcing them to consider whether to seek a further appeal or review of the failure of the appellate court to address explicitly the public law issue in the original decision.[27] There may be benefit in providing clarification that, whilst an alternative remedy is being pursued, the three month time limit for initiating judicial review proceedings does not run.

14.12   There are some indications that courts may be applying a strict interpretation of the *Goldstraw* principle, even where, in fact, no adequate alternative remedy exists.[28] The uncertainty surrounding the courts' approach in this area generates suspicion as to whether there is a hidden policy operated by the court, influenced by the policy area out of which the disputed challenge arises rather than legal principle.[29]

14.13   Whilst the requirement to exhaust alternative remedies may in practice point litigants towards the forum which is more likely to resolve finally the issues in dispute, the approach taken by the courts in recent cases may be causing unreasonable uncertainty for those seeking to bring well founded applications.

---

[23]   *R. v. Secretary of State for the Home Department, ex p. Malhi* [1991] 1 Q.B. 194; *Ibid., ex p. Oladehinde* [1991] 1 A.C. 254, 304-5. See para. 18.10 below.

[24]   H.W.R. Wade, *Administrative Law* (6th ed., 1988) p. 713.

[25]   *Leech* v. *Deputy Governor of Parkhurst Prison* [1988] A.C. 533, 567.

[26]   *Calvin* v. *Carr* [1980] A.C. 574, 594 (P.C.). We comment, however, in Part B on the many procedures used on appeals by way of rehearing, few of which actually involve a rehearing.

[27]   See paras. 18.10, 18.33 and 19.21 below. See generally C.Lewis, "The Exhaustion of Alternative Remedies", [1992] C.L.J. 138, 143.

[28]   See *R.* v. *Commissioner for the Special Purposes of the Income Tax Acts, ex p. Stipplechoice Ltd.* [1985] 2 All E.R. 465.

[29]   As perhaps has been the fear in relation to immigration cases, see *R.* v. *Secretary of State for the Home Department, ex p. Swati* [1986] 1 W.L.R. 477

Options for reform

14.14   We invite comment on the following suggestions:

(a)   The issue as to whether there is an alternative remedy which ought to be exhausted first is a matter which should be dealt with at the leave stage (whether raised by the court or the respondent), so that time and costs may not be wasted by deferring consideration until the main hearing.

(b)   Applicants for judicial review should declare on Form 86A, which initiates their application, whether any alternative avenues of appeal are available, and to state why the alternative remedy would be inadequate. If any proceedings have been instituted they should state how far these have progressed.[30]

(c)   The court should only have discretion to refuse to give leave for judicial review where it considers that an *adequate* alternative remedy exists.

(d)   There should be clarification that where an alternative remedy is being pursued, the three month time limit for initiating judicial review proceedings does not run.

14.15   We invite comment on how an amendment to R.S.C., Order 53 might be framed to give effect to these suggestions and what additional changes might be necessary in the area of time limits to eradicate any detriment to would-be applicants for judicial review who have pursued an alternative remedy before coming to court.

14.16   More generally, we invite views on the following questions:-

(a)   Has reliance on discretionary factors increased and if so, has this affected the conduct and length of proceedings?

(b)   Is the operation of the discretionary factors satisfactory?

(c)   In particular, should the merits of a particular case be relevant to the exercise of discretion to deny a remedy by way of judicial review?

(d)   Is it justifiable to give a remedy only on an historic basis?

---

[30]   In line with the dicta of Brooke J. in *R.* v. *Humberside County Council, ex p. Bogdal, The Times,* 1 June 1992.

15 SUMMARY OF ISSUES AND PROPOSALS FOR REFORM OF THE PROCEDURES AND FORMS OF RELIEF

15.1   We summarise in this section several developments in the procedure for judicial review which, in the light of the options discussed in earlier sections, we provisionally favour. This summary needs to be read in conjunction with the earlier sections which contain further detail on the options and our provisional views.

Public Policy

15.2   Judicial review inevitably raises some very difficult issues and competing interests, and it is an essential aim of procedural law to promote fairness where such competing interests come into conflict. In earlier sections of Part A we have commented on the crucial issues of legality and certainty, and of private and public interest. Whilst our summary of proposals below covers several potential areas for reform, we also encourage consultees to offer their views on the extent to which the procedure, overall, appropriately reflects the underlying purposes of the prerogative jurisdiction and a proper balance between the competing policy interests inherent in the public sphere (paragraphs 2.1-2.8).

The European dimension in administrative law reform

15.3   EC rights and obligations are directly enforceable in U.K. domestic courts. Hence, domestic procedural law is liable to be tested by whether it sufficiently enables those substantive rights and obligations to be pursued and protected through the courts. We invite consultees to comment on the possible areas in which it might be said that there is conflict between EC law principles and domestic law or between the European Convention on Human Rights and domestic law inherent in the provisions of Order 53 or in the various options for reform to which this paper refers.

15.4   *Factortame (No. 2)* poses the question of whether the principles applied in cases with a European dimension should be different to those which apply in cases involving purely domestic law issues. Whether the dual approach taken in this case can be defended in principle and whether it is acceptable as a premise for law reform, are both questions on which we invite comment (paragraphs 2.9-2.11).

Advisory declarations

15.5   We invite views as to whether it should in principle be open to the court to grant a declaration of the legal position where there is no decision to be impugned (paragraphs 2.12-2.13).

Case load management and law reform

15.6   There is only a limited scope in our review of procedure and remedies to address the problems of the numbers of cases initiated by way of judicial review. However, we have noted that some applications for judicial review stem from the absence of any form of appeal from a decision whether to a court or to a tribunal and we invite views as to whether this is satisfactory. We also invite views as to whether the number of High Court judges available to hear such cases at any one time should simply be increased. We also invite views as to whether judicial review hearings could be decentralised to High Court judges on circuit, and whether certain types of cases could be remitted to county courts or to circuit judges and Q.C.s sitting as deputy high court judges (paragraphs 2.14-2.23).

Procedural exclusivity

15.7   The principle of procedural exclusivity asserts that, as all the prerogative remedies and the remedies of declaration and injunction are available under a single procedure, and that since the procedure has been reformed to incorporate safeguards protecting the interests of the wider community, it is proper to ensure that all claims in pursuit of public law remedies are sought within the prescribed framework, so that the grant of remedies takes those wider interests into account.

15.8   We have discussed the principle of insisting on procedural exclusivity and the different options for reform. These include

(a)   abolishing the exclusivity principle so that public authorities would be exposed to the same liability to declaratory remedies as respondents in civil litigation, but accompanied by the power to strike out under R.S.C., Order 18, rule 19 on grounds of abuse of process;

(b)   developing the certainty of scope of the principle, building on the factors enunciated in *Roy* v. *Kensington and Chelsea and Westminster F.P.C.*;[1]

---

[1]   [1992] 1 A.C. 624.

(c)   facilitating transfer of issues or proceedings into or out of Order 53 so as to avoid serious detriment to cases involving a combination of public law and private law issues.

15.9   We have noted the developing trend towards limiting insistence on the use of Order 53 to claims raising issues solely of public law. We provisionally support this development and the balance which it seeks to promote, but we recognise that it does not eliminate the uncertainty and the potential for litigation over procedural issues (paragraphs 3.19-3.26).

Time Limits

15.10   At present, the primary requirement is that of promptness, the three month time limit being a secondary feature. We are influenced by the importance attached in other countries to the principle of certainty in this context, and we provisionally favour a development which would place the primary emphasis on a certain time limit.

15.11   We invite views as to whether the present three month time limit is too short. We think that the correct balance lies somewhere between three and six months. The question whether delay within the stated time limit should either bar leave or the grant of relief depends on the length of the time limit. In our view it would be rare that, within a three month period from the making of a decision, delay could fairly be argued against an applicant except possibly where substantial prejudice and hardship is proved by the respondent.

15.12   We consider that the present provisions of Section 31 of the Supreme Court Act 1981 and the provisions of Order 53, rule 4 are pointlessly confusing and that care should be taken in formulating reform to avoid splitting essential elements of the policy between the primary legislation and the rules of court (paragraphs 4.28-4.33).

The Leave Stage

15.13   We tend to the view that the leave stage in judicial review proceedings performs a necessary task in filtering out cases. However, we see scope for improving the procedure by which the leave requirement presently operates. In particular, we invite views as to whether in the intermediate category of cases mentioned by Lord Donaldson M.R., where the court is uncertain, the ex parte procedure should be amended to give respondents an opportunity to put in written representations, within a specified period. We also invite views as to whether there should be stated criteria for refusing leave, and whether there should be provision for consenting to the grant of leave (paragraphs 5.8-5.14).

Interim Relief

15.14   We support the need for the court to have effective powers of providing interim protection whilst an arguable case for judicial review is pending and, in appropriate cases, pending the determination of an application for leave paragraphs 6.32-6.33).

15.15   We do not consider that the Crown's continued immunity from interim relief is sustainable on grounds of legal principle. Following the decision of the House of Lords in *Factortame (No. 2)*, we favour reform to end the anomalous distinctions between the power to make such orders against the Crown, and against other public and local authorities, and to align the position which may if necessary be adopted in domestic and EC cases.

15.16   Of the options canvassed, we suggest that generally the most appropriate would be the introduction of a statutory power for the court to stay proceedings (not just legal proceedings but the proceedings which have prompted the application for relief) whilst an application for judicial review is pending. However we invite views on the question whether, where the legality of regulations or a decision affecting persons other than the parties to the proceeding are being challenged, it would be more appropriate to enable courts to grant an interim declaration rather than a stay (paragraphs 6.22-6.31).

Habeas Corpus

15.17   Recent cases have highlighted the disparity between habeas corpus and judicial review. Delays in the hearing of judicial review cases have led individuals, in both immigration and mental health cases, to seek to widen the traditional ambit of habeas corpus proceedings to cover grounds of review more appropriately dealt with within the framework of Order 53.

15.18   We invite consultees' views on whether reform is necessary, such that the substance and scope of habeas corpus would be left unchanged, but the Order 54 procedure modernised. We provisionally propose some amendment to Order 53 to provide the sort of interim relief that is currently being sought through habeas corpus proceedings (paragraphs 7.7-7.8).

Discovery

15.19   If courts are too cautious in the grant of discovery, and place too high a burden on the applicant to prove that the issue in respect of which discovery is sought is both arguable and needs to be determined in the proceedings, the justifications given in *O'Reilly* for requiring procedural exclusivity are weakened. While it is generally acknowledged that the principle that should be applied by the court is whether production of a document is necessary for disposing fairly of the matter, it has been suggested to us that, as the nature of judicial review proceedings means that normally not all aspects of the decision will be relevant, it would be reasonable to require the party seeking discovery to take the initiative, whether by making a specific application for discovery or otherwise. We invite views as to whether there should be a more liberal regime for discovery in judicial review proceedings, and, if so, how the particular burdens faced by the Crown can be met (paragraphs 8.9-8.12).

Standing

15.20   We consider that the general, wide approach to standing which the courts have established fits well with the public law nature of the remedies available. We consider that this test should recognise the appropriateness, in certain circumstances, of public interest challenges to rules and decisions, including general decisions. We invite comment on:

(a)   the factors to be taken into account in such cases and on the desirability of articulating them in legislation or rules of court,

(b)   whether those adversely affected by administrative action should be subject to a separate and less discretionary requirement of standing,

(c)   whether there should be a presumption as to legislative intent to act as a long stop where the statute is inconclusive and, if so, what it should be, and

(d)   the relevance of the seriousness or widespread nature of the illegality alleged.

15.21   We also seek views on the way in which standing is considered at the leave stage, whether it should be more fully considered then, and whether deliberation of the issue of standing at the main hearing encourages courts to focus too much on the merits of applications (paragraphs 9.19-9.28).

Restitution

15.22   We propose that it should be permissible for an applicant to join a restitutionary claim for repayment of money unlawfully demanded, with an application for judicial review. The court should be able to make an order or to give directions for further consideration of the restitutionary claim as appropriate in a similar manner to that which currently applies in relation to claims for damages (paragraph 10.3).

Costs

15.23 The Crown's interest in the principle of legality and the proper supervision of public decision making bodies is not reflected in the costs rules in Crown proceedings. We invite views on whether, where leave has been granted, the usual rule that costs should follow the event might be departed from (paragraphs 11.8-11.14).

Appeals from refusal of substantive applications for judicial review

15.24 We tend to the view that any appeal from the decision of the High Court ought to be cast by reference to the wider general importance of the disputed issue. The options would be either to introduce a leave requirement for all appeals to the Court of Appeal (Civil Division) with the primary ground for appeal being that the appeal raises a point of law of general public importance, or a straight exclusion of appeals except where the High Court certifies that there is a point of general public importance. In order to bring the routes of appeal into alignment consideration might also be given to allowing appeals in criminal causes to the Court of Appeal (Criminal Division) on the same basis.

15.25 We consider that there may be scope for improving the arrangements for the first consideration and renewal of applications for leave, and for resolving, where there is an overlap between the power to renew and to appeal, which is the proper procedure (paragraphs 12.8-12.11).

Substitution of order for that of the lower court

15.26 In general we consider that the lower court, tribunal or administrative body has the continuing responsibility for exercising the jurisdiction which has been expressly conferred on it. The duty to redetermine in the light of the High Court's finding is part of that responsibility. We invite views, however, on whether there is scope for allowing the High Court to substitute its order where the grounds for review arise out of error of law (paragraphs 13.1-13.4).

Discretionary nature of remedies

15.27 We believe that it is normally incompatible with the court's reviewing function for the merits of a case to be taken into account in exercising discretion whether to grant relief. We invite views as to the role of discretion in the exercise of judicial review at the leave stage, when interim relief is being considered, and in the context of standing and delay. We also invite views as to the appropriateness of exercising the court's discretion to grant relief only on an historic footing (paragraphs 14.2-14.5).

15.28   The issue as to whether alternative remedies must be exhausted first should be addressed when the application for judicial review is first initiated. Form 86A might be adapted for this purpose (14.14(b)).

15.29   The requirement to exhaust alternative remedies cannot properly be regarded as a principle to be applied in all save exceptional circumstances. The approach which the court should adopt should be to consider whether the potential alternative remedy is adequate.

15.30   We invite comment how an amendment to R.S.C. Order 53 might be framed to give effect to these suggestions and whether there should be provision that the three month time limit for judicial review applications does not run whilst an appellate remedy is being pursued (paragraphs 14.11,14.15).

PART B

STATUTORY APPEALS AND APPLICATIONS TO THE HIGH COURT

FROM OTHER BODIES

16   **INTRODUCTION**

16.1   In this Part we consider whether there is scope for rationalising the great array of statutory provisions which give access to the High Court on appeal or application from an inferior court, tribunal or other body.[1] It is often said that the statutory provisions which regulate the manner in which administrative and adjudicatory decisions are taken are necessarily very specific to the context for which they were designed,[2] and this is a factor which must be borne in mind in considering the extent to which simplification and harmonisation is possible.

16.2   The number of statutory appeal provisions is very great, as can be seen from the list contained in Annex 2.[3] It would be impracticable for us to consider all these statutory provisions or to address the issues which have arisen in relation to individual provisions in detail. For this reason our approach in this Part differs from that adopted in Part A for judicial review. Instead of an analysis of individual problematic issues, we begin with a short outline of the main avenues of appeal and application to the High Court. This is followed by an account of the relevant procedures aimed at testing the scope for overall simplification,[4] as opposed to the piecemeal repair of problems with individual statutory provisions.

---

[1]   Provisions for direct appeal from tribunals to the Court of Appeal, for instance from the Lands Tribunal and the Social Security Commissioners, do not fall within item 10(b) of our programme (Fifth Programme of Law Reform (1991), Law Com 200).

[2]   Robson, *Justice and Administrative Law* (3rd ed., 1951); J.A. Farmer, *Tribunals & Government* (1974), Preface.

[3]   Annex 2 lists the existing enactments providing for appeals or applications to the High Court.

[4]   Sir Harry Woolf, "A Hotchpotch of Appeals - the Need for a Blender", (1988) 7 C.J.Q. 44; "Judicial Review: A Possible Programme for Reform", [1992] P.L. 221, 229.

16.3 Accordingly, consultees may well find that there is no reference to or discussion of individual issues which arise in the particular context with which they are familiar. What we are primarily seeking to elicit at this stage are views on the general question of rationalisation. However, we are also interested in knowing about the features of individual procedures which are thought by those directly involved in a particular context to be either problematic or beneficial. We invite consultees to comment on these matters and on our more general summary of issues aimed at testing the scope for rationalisation and simplification. If there is support for the principle of rationalisation, we also seek consultees' views as to how to take the matter forward.

Applications to Quash

16.4 Applications to quash provide a closely defined procedure under which the decision or order of a statutory body, tribunal or Minister may be challenged on the grounds that an order is "not within the powers" of the Act (i.e. illegality) or that "any requirement" of the Act "has not been complied with". Their main characteristic is the exclusive nature of the right of legal challenge. They provide the only way in which a decision may be challenged and quashed, and set a strict timetable (usually six weeks or 42 days, but sometimes longer[5]) within which challenges may be made.

16.5 Applications to quash are commonly referred to as "statutory review" and are often subject to a "preclusive clause". These terms identify two main purposes of the procedure: firstly, the issue which may be challenged relates not to the merits of the decision but to whether it fell within the lawful powers of the decision-maker and whether there were procedural irregularities of major significance. Secondly, the statute in which they are contained is primarily concerned with limiting legal challenges to decisions, except to the extent specifically authorised. It often provides that except as provided in the statute, "the validity of an order shall not be questioned in any legal proceedings whatsoever".[6]

Statutory Appeals

16.6 This term in a general sense covers all the field under review in Part B, but can be broken down into the three main procedures of appeals by way of rehearing, appeals on a point of law and appeals by case stated.

   16.6.1 Appeals by way of rehearing. These give the High Court power to reconsider the disputed decision on its merits. They often relate to decisions of a professional disciplinary body, where the consequence of an adverse decision may involve the loss of a career.

---

[5] e.g. Medicines Act 1968, s. 107 (three months).

[6] e.g. Wildlife and Countryside Act 1981, para. 7(4) to Schedule 11.

16.6.2 Appeals on a point of law. These provide a forum for correcting errors of law and keeping inferior courts and tribunals in touch with the general principles of law, legality and natural justice. In general, the High Court has wide powers on hearing statutory appeals. Subject to any special limitations prescribed in the statutory provision, it may substitute its own decision, amend, quash, remit the case to the lower tribunal, or give its opinion on the problematic point of law. The procedures which it can adopt incorporate a broader discretion than is available under applications to quash.

16.6.3 Appeals by way of case stated. These differ significantly from other statutory appeals and we consider them separately. Appeals by way of case stated are most common in relation to appeals from magistrates' courts and Crown Courts, and from some long established tribunals where the factual background is complicated and is set out for the benefit of the High Court.

16.7 References to the High Court are often an adjunct to statutory provisions for appeals on a point of law or by way of case stated. The tribunal, of its own volition or at the instance of the parties, can refer a question of law to the High Court for its opinion at an interlocutory stage.

Crown Office Proceedings

16.8 A high percentage (but not all) of the proceedings under discussion in this paper are handled by the Crown Office and listed for hearing in the Crown Office List. R.S.C., Order 57 prescribes rules relevant to all Divisional Court proceedings in each High Court division. For Queen's Bench matters, proceedings will be processed by the Crown Office if the jurisdiction is conferred on a Divisional Court or a single judge relating to committals, judicial review, habeas corpus and in certain criminal proceedings.[7] Proceedings in the Crown Office List are heard by 18 specially nominated High Court judges.

16.9 The Crown Office is the appropriate office for many appeals to the High Court from inferior courts, tribunals and persons, except where jurisdiction is assigned to a different Division. It also handles appeals by way of case stated in criminal causes and matters as well as in respect of decisions by Ministers and tribunals. With certain exceptions these are all assigned to a Queen's Bench Divisional Court or a single Queen's Bench judge. The Crown Office is also responsible for applications and appeals to the High Court under Order 94, generally speaking for all applications to quash (other than those assigned to another division) and certain other applications.[8]

---

[7] For the Chancery Division the appropriate office is Chancery Chambers; for the Family Division, the Principal Registry; proceedings in the Queen's Bench relating to admiralty go to the Admiralty and Commercial registry.

[8] See O. 94, rr. 4-15, and O. 111.

17.1   Statutory applications to quash are most frequently incorporated in legislation relating to land use planning, highways, compulsory acquisition of land and government licensing.[1] This is not because of any inherent suitability of the procedure for investigating decisions made in these areas; rather, it is the form of statutory provision commonly adopted where a vital policy of the statute is to provide finality to challenges to decisions made, so that those charged with implementation can carry out their statutory duties without risk of legal upset.

17.2   The purpose of applications to quash, though never expressly referred to in statute, was commented on in the Franks Report.[2] It considered that, given safeguards covering the manner in which matters of fact were established and could be corrected, appeals on matters of fact were not necessary, and that they would, in effect, introduce an appeal on merits. The Committee considered that the application to quash on grounds of ultra vires or procedural defect adequately covered the need for an appeal on a question of law.[3] Although the courts can take a wide view of their powers in proceedings by statutory review[4] and the grounds are similar to those for judicial review, they are not precisely the same. Statutory review for non-compliance with "any requirement" of the statute generally requires that the interests of the applicant must have been "substantially prejudiced" and may therefore be narrower than judicial review. However, where substantial prejudice is established, statutory review may permit relief for breach of a directory requirement.[5]

17.3   There are many similarities in the manner in which the statutory provisions are drafted. Legal challenges are limited to the extent provided by the statute: thus it

---

[1]   See for example the Housing Act 1930, s. 11, now consolidated in the Housing Act 1985, Schedules 11 and 12, and see Annex 2 below.

[2]   Report of the Franks Committee on Administrative Tribunals and Enquiries (1957), Cmnd. 218.

[3]   *Ibid.*, para. 359.

[4]   It is generally accepted that "not within the powers of this Act" authorises review for unreasonableness and irrelevant considerations, for error of law, including misinterpretation of statute, and probably for acting on no evidence: *Ashbridge Investments Ltd.* v. *Minister of Housing and Local Government* [1965] 1 W.L.R. 1320, 1326G-H; *R.* v. *Secretary of State for the Environment, ex p. Upton Brickworks Ltd. and R.P. 120 Ltd.* [1992] J.P.L. 1044, 1045.

[5]   H.W.R.Wade, Administrative Law (6th ed., 1988), pp. 739-743. See R.J.F. Gordon, *Crown Office Proceedings* (1990), paras. G1-022 -036 for situations in which judicial review may nevertheless be available.

provides the jurisdiction and limits the power of other forms of legal challenge. The area of circumscribed legal challenge has to be clearly identified. Strict time limits are prescribed and standing to challenge is specified. There is no leave requirement. The grounds for challenge show that it is the validity of the order that is liable to challenge, not the merits. The order can be suspended whilst the challenge is pending. The remedy is that the order or decision is quashed.

17.4   Section 2 of this paper adverts to the competing public policy interests influencing this area of law. An extreme example of the conflicting interests of an aggrieved person and the public interest in speed and certainty in implementing decisions for the benefit of the wider community can be seen in the strict application of the time limits for bringing applications to quash. In *R. v. Secretary of State for the Environment, ex p. Ostler*[6] it was held that challenges to compulsory purchase orders could not be made after expiry of the six week time limit even where the grounds for the application to quash related to bad faith verging on fraud. In the field of compulsory purchase, in particular, the reality of these conflicting interests becomes harshly apparent.

Procedure

17.5   Applications to quash are brought by way of originating motion in the High Court. This form of proceedings is common where the material facts are not in dispute and do not need to be pleaded. The focus from the outset is on the grounds for challenging the decision, and these must be set out in the notice. There are other provisions[7] relating to the respondents to be served, and to the filing and use of evidence. R.S.C. Order 8 also applies, governing such general matters as the making of ex parte motions and the adjournment of the hearing of any motion.[8] What is unclear, however, is the scope of orders which the court has jurisdiction to make and the dividing line between what is procedural and what is substantive in terms of the matters which may be asked for as an interlocutory step in proceedings.

---

[6]   [1977] Q.B. 122. See also *Smith* v. *East Elloe Rural District Council* [1956] A.C. 736 and on the exclusivity of the remedy *R. v. Cornwall County Council, ex p. Huntington* [1992] 3 All E.R. 566.

[7]   Primarily in Order 94.

[8]   Generally to resolve interlocutory matters before the matter is ready for final hearing.

18.1   A right of appeal to the High Court exists from a wide range of inferior courts, tribunals and other bodies or persons, including Ministers and Government Departments. The main groups of tribunals and inquiries are those from which an appeal on a point of law lies by or under statute, predominantly the Tribunals and Inquiries Act 1992, section 11 and schedule 1, a consolidating measure which replaced the Tribunals and Inquiries Act 1971, section 13(1) and schedule 1.[1]

18.2   There are different types of appeals and the differences relate both to what may be appealed and to procedure. It is no simple matter to define the purposes of such appeals, nor to correlate them to a particular form of procedure designed to facilitate the examination of the issues in dispute under the appeals. Generally speaking, there are two main procedures: appeals by rehearing and appeals on a point of law, both covered by the provisions of R.S.C., Order 55. After we have considered these, we then examine a third important form of appeal procedure: appeal by case stated.

18.3   R.S.C., Order 55 deals with such matters as the judicial officer hearing the issue, service on the other parties to the dispute and the body appealed from, and the time limits. Unlike applications to quash, the bringing of an appeal does not stay the operation of the disputed order unless the court or body so directs. The difference between appeals and applications to quash is most apparent in Order 55, rule 7 which states the court's order-making powers. The court can hear further evidence and can determine in what manner to receive such evidence. The court may give any judgment or decision or make any order which ought to have been given by the body appealed from and make such further order as the case may require or may remit the matter with the opinion of the Court for rehearing and determination by that body.

18.4   Several other Rules of the Supreme Court contain specific rules for particular forms of appeal.[2] Order 57 (Divisional Court proceedings) also applies: so too do the more general provisions of the Rules of the Supreme Court where necessary, for example, in relation to interlocutory procedure or for security for costs and costs rules.

---

[1]   As from 1 October 1992. The 1971 Act was itself a consolidation of the 1958 Act and later developments.

[2]   For example, appeals from V.A.T. tribunals (O. 91, r. 6); Consumer Credit Licensing Appeals under the Consumer Credit Act 1974 (O. 94, r.10A); appeals from the Pensions Appeal Tribunal (O. 101); under the Town and Country Planning Act 1990 (O. 94, r.12); and appeals and applications for a declaration under the Local Government Finance Act 1982 (O. 98).

Appeals by way of rehearing

18.5   The purpose of such appeals is to confer on the appellate court the power to reverse the decision of the lower court, if it considers that it was wrong. In such appeals, the High Court is not limited to points of law. In the case of *Hughes* v. *Architects' Registration Council of the United Kingdom*,[3] the purpose of the appeal procedure was explained.

> "It has been held by this court that a section in these terms [Section 9 of the Architects (Registration) Act 1931] confers a right of appeal as wide as one from a judge to the Court of Appeal: see *Allender* v. *Royal College of Veterinary Surgeons* [1951] 2 All E.R. 859. While an appellate court will always attach great importance to the finding of a lower court, especially on findings of fact, if, in their opinion, the decision below is wrong they must give effect to their opinion and reverse it."[4]

18.6   Although Order 55 refers to appeals as being by way of rehearing, it is misleading to believe that all such appeals in fact involve a rehearing. The court looks at the case as presented to the original body and its judgment, for which purpose the record of the original proceedings is required.[5] The court can inquire into the circumstances and is unfettered in any investigation which it may think right to make in order to ascertain the facts.[6]

18.7   Appeals to the High Court from magistrates' courts are statutory. In some cases a particular statute confers the right of appeal, but where no specific right of appeal is conferred, an appeal by way of case stated may be made if the decision or order was wrong in law or in excess of jurisdiction.[7] Apart from appeals in criminal causes, an important element of the appeal jurisdiction from magistrates' courts to the High Court relates to decisions in family proceedings. The Children Act 1989 altered the procedure for appeals from magistrates' courts to the High Court, largely replacing use of case stated procedure by a statutory appeal provision.[8]

---

3   [1957] 2 Q.B. 550, (*per* Lord Goddard C.J.).

4   *Ibid.*, 558.

5   O.55, r. 7(4).

6   *Stock* v. *Central Midwives Board* [1915] 3 K.B. 756, 763.

7   The statutory provisions for appeal by case stated are contained in the Magistrates' Courts Act 1980, s. 111, and the Magistrates' Courts Rules 1981 (S.I. 1981, No. 552).

8   Children Act 1989, s. 94(1).

18.8   The Franks Committee considered that there was a need for appeals on points of law and recommended that the procedure should in general take the form of an appeal on a point of law, rather than certiorari.[9] It recommended that appeals on matters of fact and merits should go to an appellate level of the specialist tribunal, not to the High Court.[10]

18.9   This policy was implemented in the Tribunals and Inquiries Act 1958, and is now reflected in section 11 of the 1992 consolidation, which subjects many tribunals to an appeal on a point of law and remains the most important statutory provision on this subject.[11] Rights of appeal to the High Court from a tribunal or other body on a point of law are also conferred, without reference to the Tribunals and Inquiries Act, in other areas. The tribunals or other bodies whose decisions may be appealed are not confined to those subject to the supervision of the Council on Tribunals under the 1992 Act.[12]

18.10   In general rights of appeal on a point of law have included the right to raise jurisdictional questions,[13] and indeed, since errors of law generally go to jurisdiction,[14] any other approach would leave almost no scope for appeals.[15] There are, however, some cases in which a more restrictive approach appears to have been taken.[16] It has also been said, albeit in the context of a right of appeal to an immigration adjudicator (rather than the High Court), that a right of appeal where "there is no power" to make an order did not empower the appellate body to give relief for mistake of law or fact, procedural irregularity, or *Wednesbury*

---

[9]   Report of the Franks Committee on Administrative Tribunals and Enquiries (1957), Cmnd. 218, para. 107.

[10]   *Ibid.*, paras. 105 and 106.

[11]   Decisions of the Director General of Fair Trading in relation to the grant of consumer credit licences and of the Secretary of State relating to off-street parking regulations are also subject to appeal on a point of law under section 11(1).

[12]   Sections 1, 5-8, and 10 of, and Schedule 1 to, the 1992 Act.

[13]   *R.* v. *I.R.C., ex p. Preston* [1985] A.C. 835, at 862; *Arsenal F.C.* v. *Ende* [1977] Q.B. 100, at 116.

[14]   *Pearlman* v. *Keepers and Governors of Harrow School* [1979] Q.B. 56; *Re Racal Communications Ltd.* [1981] A.C. 374.

[15]   H.W.R. Wade, *Administrative Law* (6th ed.,1988), p. 946.

[16]   e.g. *Chapman* v. *Earl* [1968] 1 W.L.R. 1315 (relief only by way of certiorari); *Henry Moss Ltd.* v. *Commissioners of Customs and Excise* [1981] 2 All E.R. 86, 90.

unreasonableness.[17] One reason given, however, has implications for other forms of appeal. It was stated that for an appellate body to have similar powers to those exercisable by the High Court on judicial review "would be an unnecessary and potentially embarrassing overlap of jurisdiction".[18]

Appeals by way of case stated

18.11 The main categories of appeals by way of case stated are from the magistrates' courts to the High Court in criminal causes or matters, or from the Crown Court to the High Court, or from specialist tribunals. The right of appeal by way of case stated serves a similar purpose to the right of appeal on a point of law, and in fact, most appeals by way of case stated are limited to points of law. However, the question arises as to whether statement of a case serves a further and distinct purpose.

18.12 Section 11 of the Tribunals and Inquiries Act 1992 provides that the person seeking to appeal on a point of law may either appeal to the High Court or, according as rules of court may provide, require the tribunal to state and sign a case for the opinion of the court. The procedures are alternative, not cumulative, and the statute provides no guidance as to whether this division of appeal routes was meant to indicate a distinction of substance or not.

18.13 The Franks Committee was dissatisfied with the case stated procedure which in 1957 was the established procedure for appeal from such tribunals as provided for an appeal on a point of law. The process of drafting a case was seen as imposing a severe burden on tribunals where parties were not represented by Counsel. The statement of case was considered unnecessary where the decision notice adequately set out the facts and reasons. Case stated was not considered satisfactory where the issue under appeal related to whether there was any evidence on which the tribunal could properly have come to the decision. The Committee concluded

> "... that the simplest, cheapest and most expeditious method would be a straight appeal to the court just as in the case of appeals on law from the County Court to the Court of Appeal."[19]

---

[17]   *R. v. Secretary of State for the Home Department, ex p. Malhi* [1991] 1 Q.B. 194, 207-8, 211; *R. v. Secretary of State of the Home Department ex p. Oladehinde* [1991] 1 A.C. 254.

[18]   *Ex p. Oladehinde* [1991] 1 A.C. 254 at 305 (Lord Griffiths). See also *Ex p. Malhi* [1991] 1 Q.B. 194 at 211 (Stuart-Smith L.J. who mentioned that, unlike judicial review, the appellate jurisdiction was not subject to a requirement of leave.).

[19]   Report of the Franks Committee on Administrative Tribunals and Enquiries (1957), Cmnd. 218, para. 113.

18.14 The Committee was, therefore, introducing an innovation in providing for an alternative to case stated as the preferred appeal mechanism. This started the trend, which the Council on Tribunals still advocates, away from case stated to a straight appeal on a point of law for tribunals and inquiries governed by the 1992 Act.

18.15 As against the criticisms of the procedure noted above, the strengths of appeals by way of case stated may be identified as follows. A case stated may be suitable where parties are not represented at the original hearing or where there are complex factual issues. It not only provides the appellate court with the decision reached but relates the facts and contentions of the parties to that decision. As distinct from other forms of appeal where the court initially has only the appellant's stated grounds, a case stated clarifies both the findings of fact which are not open to appeal, and the issue which is the subject of the appeal. It achieves early concentration on the issue under appeal at the cost of additional effort in the process of the formulation of the case. In *R. v. Crown Court at Ipswich, ex p. Baldwin*, the Divisional Court said that the case stated procedure was the only convenient and proper way in which to put before the higher court a case which "bristles with factual difficulties".[20]

18.16 There is authority as regards magistrates' courts and the Crown Court that the court may refuse a party's application to state a case if it considers the application frivolous,[21] though the High Court may in a proper case force the lower court to state a case.[22] This limited power of refusal is a distinguishing feature: it provides a check on the number of frivolous applications reaching the higher court, but it also operates as a curb on the appellant's right of appeal. There is no express statutory power in the High Court to force a Crown Court (on appeal from a magistrates' court) to amend a case, although a Divisional Court may remit a case to the Crown Court for it to be re-stated.[23] We invite consultees views on whether this situation requires rectification.

Procedure

18.17 R.S.C., Order 56 applies to appeals by way of case stated, modified, in some cases, by other rules relevant to the particular statute, or by Order made under the statute. The rules relating to case stated by the Crown Court are contained in Order 56, rules 1 to 4A; those relating to magistrates are contained in Order 56, rules 5 and 6; and

---

[20]   [1981] 1 All E.R. 596, 597b,c.

[21]   C.C.R. 1971, r. 21(3); Magistrates' Courts Act 1980, s. 111(5).

[22]   For Ministers and Tribunals etc., under R.S.C., O. 56, r.8; for Crown Courts under the Supreme Court Act 1981, s.29(3); for magistrates' courts under the Magistrates' Courts Act 1980, s.111(6).

[23]   Order 56/1/8.

those relating to Ministers, tribunals and other bodies are (mainly) contained in Order 56, rules 7 to 13. The rules deal with the assignment of different forms of appeal to either a Divisional Court or a single judge, and the power to require any such Minister or tribunal etc. to state such a case is explicitly stated.[24] There are close similarities with Order 55 in that Order 56 sets out the general provisions,[25] but there are some significant differences between case stated appeals from the Crown Court and magistrates' court, and cases stated from Ministers etc.

Cases stated from the Crown Court and Magistrates' Courts

18.18 Section 28 of the Supreme Court Act 1981, R.S.C., Order 56, rules 1 to 6, and the provisions of rule 26 of the Crown Court Rules 1982[26] and rules 76 to 81 of the Magistrates' Court Rules 1981[27] make provision for the manner of application for the statement of a case from the Crown Court, and from magistrates' courts.[28]

18.19 As regards the Crown Court, section 28 of the 1981 Act provides that

> "(1) Subject to subsection (2),[29] any order, judgment or other decision of the Crown Court may be questioned by any party to the proceedings, on the ground that it is wrong in law or is in excess of jurisdiction, by applying to the Crown Court to have a case stated by that court for the opinion of the High Court."

The phrase "any order, judgment or other decision" has been held to mean that the Crown Court cannot state a case before the proceedings have been concluded.[30]

---

[24]   R.S.C., O. 56, r.7(1) and (2).

[25]   As with Order 55, Order 56 defers to any express provisions to the contrary which may govern a particular case.

[26]   S.I. 1982, No. 1109.

[27]   S.I. 1981, No. 552.

[28]   The Notes to the Supreme Court Practice 1993, vol. 1, paras. 56/1/1-9 and 56/5/1-12 provide a useful commentary on the procedures relevant to statement of case from the Crown Court and magistrates' courts to the High Court, from which much of the text in this Part of the paper is drawn.

[29]   The exceptions in subsection (2) relate to judgments and orders relating to trial on indictment and certain decisions relating to licensing, betting and local government matters where the decision of the Crown Court is final.

[30]   *Loade* v. *Director of Public Prosecutions* [1990] C.O.D. 58 (Div. Ct.)(in a criminal cause or matter). As regards civil proceedings, the court ought to be cautious about agreeing to state a case before the conclusion of the Crown Court proceedings: *R.* v. *Secretary of State for Environment, ex p. the Royal Borough of Kensington and Chelsea* (1987) 19 H.L.R. 161.

However, this section does not provide the High Court with any specific powers of disposal. With respect to the courts of quarter sessions, the High Court had powers to draw any inference of fact or make any judgment or order which the inferior court might have drawn or made and the power to remit the case to that court for a re-hearing.[31] In abolishing the courts of quarter sessions and replacing them with the new Crown Court the section containing these powers was repealed without being replaced by an equivalent provision for the new court.[32]   We are provisionally in favour of an amendment to section 28 of the Supreme Court Act to confirm the High Court's powers of disposal over cases stated from the Crown Court.

18.20   For magistrates' courts, the appeal provision is contained in section 111 of the Magistrates' Court Act 1980. Subsection (1) provides

> "(1) Any person who was a party to any proceedings before a magistrates' court or is aggrieved by the conviction, order, determination or other proceedings of the court may question the proceeding on the ground that it is wrong in law or is in excess of jurisdiction by applying to the justices... to state a case for the opinion of the High Court on the question of law or jurisdiction involved..."

The powers given to the High Court in dealing with cases stated from a magistrates' court are still those contained in the Summary Jurisdiction Act 1857.[33] These powers could be re-introduced into the legislative mainstream in combination with the amendment suggested above in respect of the analogous powers for the Crown Court, as a single new provision.[34]

18.21   One distinction between Crown Court procedure and that governing magistrates' courts case stated is that the right to appeal from the Crown Court is given to "any party to the proceedings", whereas under section 111(1) of the 1980 Act an appeal may be made by any person "... who was a party to any proceeding before a magistrates' court or is aggrieved by the conviction, order, determination or other proceeding of the court...". A further difference is that the time limit for applying for a case stated in magistrates' courts (but not for the Crown Court) is prescribed in

---

[31]   Section 25 of the Supreme Court of Judicature (Consolidation) Act 1925.

[32]   Section 56(4) and schedule 11 (Part IV) of the Courts Act 1971.

[33]   20 & 21 Vict. c.43, sections 6 and 7.

[34]   Sections 6 and 7 of the Summary Jurisdiction Act 1857 would be substantively retained whilst the rest of the remaining portions (sections 10,12,15) of the Statute would be repealed.

the statute and is not capable of extension.[35] Another difference is that the power of the High Court to remit a case to the Crown Court to be re-stated is based on case law,[36] whereas in relation to magistrates' courts cases, the power is statutory.[37]

Case Stated by Ministers, tribunals and other administrative bodies

18.22 Appeals are brought by way of originating motion. Jurisdiction is generally assigned to a single judge of the Queen's Bench Division, unless other rules or statute provide to the contrary. In common with other forms of appeal by way of case stated, the notice of motion sets out the applicant's contentions or question of law. Other matters which are expressly covered are the time limits for appeals, the persons to be served, the proper judicial officer before whom any interlocutory proceedings are to be heard, amendments to the case, and the right of the Minister to appear and be heard.

18.23 One distinctive feature of the rules relating to appeals by way of case stated from Ministers, tribunals and other administrative bodies, as distinct from those arising from Crown Courts or magistrates courts, is the provision for an application to be made to require the Minister, tribunal or other body to state a case, which may be needed where the Minister has refused to state a case.[38]

18.24 Another distinction is that only in relation to cases stated from Ministers, tribunals and other administrative bodies is it envisaged that a case may be stated at an interlocutory stage (sometimes referred to as a special case), and not from the Crown Court or magistrates' courts. As mentioned above, the provision in the Tribunals and Inquiries Act 1992 countenances the possibility that such bodies may refuse to state a case in the course of proceedings, so the right to state a special case is limited to that extent. In considering whether a right to apply for a special case exists, the would-be appellant has to consider the terms of the statute creating the right of appeal.

18.25 There are other rules of court, enactments and subordinate legislation relevant to the procedure for case stated.[39] To these must be added the particular regulations relevant to the particular Tribunal's procedures provided either in specific legislation

---

[35] Magistrates' Courts Act 1980, s. 111(2); *R.* v. *Clerkenwell Metropolitan Stipendiary Magistrates, ex p. D.P.P.* [1984] Q.B. 821.

[36] *Vyner* v. *Wirral R.D.C* (1909) 73 J.P. 242.

[37] Summary Jurisdiction Act 1867, s.7.

[38] R.S.C., O. 56, r.8.

[39] Particular provisions are contained in Order 94 for the Agricultural Land Tribunal, tribunals mentioned in the Tribunals and Inquiries Act 1971, 13(1), the Mental Health Tribunal and the Social Securities Acts 1975 to 1986.

or in regulations made under that legislation.[40] There is no comprehensive list, other than those listed in Orders 93 and 94, detailing which tribunals etc. are covered by the alternative appeal or case stated appeal procedures.

Miscellaneous provisions for appeals

18.26 There are miscellaneous forms of statutory appeal and case stated which do not conform with the generalisations set out earlier.

Appeals not restricted to points of law

18.27 Certain provisions provide that an appeal may be made on questions of fact or law,[41] or where there are mixed questions of fact and law, or where the matters are "likely to be substantially confined to questions of law".[42] In the case of the Taxes Management Act 1970, section 100C, there is provision for appeal from the determination of the Commissioners of the Inland Revenue that a penalty is payable. The powers of the High Court on appeal extend not only to questions of law, but also (on appeal by the defendant) to the amount of the penalty, in which case the High Court also has power to reduce, or increase, the penalty.

Further appeals to High Court from inferior courts and bodies acting as appellate bodies

18.28 There are also some statutory provisions whereby a further appeal to the High Court may be made from the decision (made on appeal from another body) of a county court.[43] The Pilotage Act 1983, section 26, provides for a further appeal from the decision of a magistrates' court on a question of law and fact to the High Court.

18.29 The High Court, under certain provisions, provides a further avenue of appeal after an initial decision has been the subject of an appeal to a statutory tribunal, or to the appropriate Secretary of State, and the appellant is still dissatisfied. Often, in these

---

[40] For example, there are rules as to the proper procedure for obtaining the statement of the case from the tribunal appealed from to be found in the Pensions Appeal Tribunal (England and Wales) Rules 1980, rr. 25-32: S.I. 1980, No. 1120.

[41] Copyright, Designs and Patents Act 1988, s.251 (references and appeals on design right matters). Appeals go from the Comptroller General to the Patents Court which is part of the Chancery Division of the High Court.

[42] Inheritance Act 1984, s.222; Stamp Duty Reserve Tax Regulations 1986, (S.I. 1986, No. 1711) r. 8.

[43] Parish and Community Meetings (Polls) Rules 1987, S.I. 1987, No. 1, Schedule.

circumstances, the right of appeal to the High Court is limited to points of law,[44] and the matter has to be remitted to the tribunal to be disposed of there, in the light of the High Court's opinion.

Shared jurisdiction between inferior courts and bodies and the High Court

18.30 Some statutes provide that jurisdiction is shared in contested matters between the High Court and the inferior court or tribunal. This is so for the Comptroller General of Patents, Designs and Trade Marks,[45] election courts[46] and the Charity Commissioners.[47] There are similar provisions in relation to courts exercising insolvency jurisdiction under the Insolvency Act and regarding children's proceedings under the Children Act 1989.

Powers to refer issues to the High Court for its opinion

18.31 We have referred to the existence of statutory provisions which enable issues to be raised by way of seeking the opinion of the High Court. The boundary between those powers of reference which are appeals, and those which are more appropriately regarded as references on a particular issue for the court's opinion, is necessarily blurred. It reflects the variety of situations in which the desire for a ruling by a higher court may arise before lower courts.

18.32 In some circumstances these provisions may properly be regarded as appeals, in that they follow on from a disputed finding made by the tribunal. But other provisions are cast in terms of a power to refer, either at the instance of the inferior decision-maker or at the request (or insistence) of the parties.[48] The power to refer may be initiated by the court of its own motion, irrespective of the views of the parties. In such cases the High Court is in effect providing guidance on a point of law on which the tribunal

---

[44]   e.g. Banking Act 1987 s.31 (where an appeal lies from the appeal tribunal to the High Court on a question of law); Building Societies Act 1986, s. 49.

[45]   Copyright, Designs and Patents Act 1988, s. 251 (power of comptroller to order proceedings or any question to be referred to the High Court).

[46]   See Representation of the People Act 1983, s. 146 (special case for determination of the High Court). The appeal proceedings are commenced by way of petition, and may be raised at either an interim stage or after the election court's determination. Leave of the High Court is required.

[47]   Charities Act 1960, s. 18, which provides concurrent jurisdiction with the High Court for certain purposes. The Charity Commissioners should cede jurisdiction to the High Court where the contentious nature of the matter so requires or if there is a special question of law or fact to be determined.

[48]   See, for example, Copyright, Designs and Patents Act 1988, s. 251.

may be troubled in a particular case. The power of reference enables a specific point to be determined without the lower court losing jurisdiction over the main subject matter of the dispute.

18.33   An issue which has recently emerged concerns the limitations as to what types of errors of law may be determined within the statutorily conferred jurisdiction of an appellate body.   The decision in *Chief Adjudication Officer* v. *Foster*[49] recently highlighted a lacuna in the power of a lower tribunal to determine on appeal a dispute as to the vires of regulations. The Court of Appeal held that it was not open to the Social Security Commissioner hearing an appeal from the decision of a Social Security Appeal Tribunal to hold that the regulations underpinning the Tribunal's decision were invalid. The scope of appellate jurisdiction into errors of law related to errors made by the decision maker as to the correct interpretation of the law, not an error in the law itself. The Court of Appeal held that power to quash regulations on the grounds of invalidity was a remedy only open to a court exercising supervisory jurisdiction by way of judicial review.

18.34   This case has drawn criticism[50] due to its restricted interpretation of the role of the powers of the appellate level of tribunals to deal with errors of law.   It has implications for all courts whose appellate jurisdiction is conferred by statute: thus it could apply equally to the High Court's appellate jurisdiction, as to the Social Security Commissioner and the Court of Appeal.[51]   A Court hearing a statutory appeal could not, arguably, quash or declare the regulations invalid outside the framework of an application for judicial review.

18.35   The facility for referring a disputed question of law to the High Court for its opinion may assist in the resolution of the difficulty posed by the *Foster* decision. The quashing of a regulation is a matter which has wider public implications and would fall squarely within the field of judicial review, but the power to determine whether a regulation is ultra vires may be a necessary element in the appellate tribunal's determination as to whether there has been an error of law. It might, therefore be appropriate to consider conferring power on an appellate tribunal to refer such an issue of illegality to the High Court for its opinion as to the issue of illegality.

---

[49]   [1992] Q.B. 31 (C.A.). This is currently under appeal to the House of Lords.

[50]   D. Feldman, "Review, Appeal and Jurisdictional Confusion", (1992) 108 L.Q.R. 45; A.W. Bradley, "Administrative Justice and Judicial Review: Taking Tribunals Seriously?", [1992] P.L. 185. Cf. Sir Harry Woolf, "Judicial Review: A Possible Programme for Reform", [1992] P.L. 221, 232.

[51]   See also para. 18.10 above.

18.36   The Insolvency Act 1986 and the rules made under it make provision for appeals from the decision of a county court judge (or district judge) to a single judge of the High Court.[52] The procedure on such appeals is governed, not by R.S.C., Order 55, but by R.S.C., Order 59.[53] This emphasises the similarity between the approach to be adopted by the High Court on hearing such appeals and that adopted by the Court of Appeal.

---

[52]   Insolvency Act 1986, s. 375(2) (individual insolvency); Insolvency Rules 1986, S.I. 1986, No. 1925, rule 7.47 (company insolvency). The current procedure for individual insolvency replaced the procedure under the Bankruptcy Act 1914 whereby appeals went to the Divisional Court of the Chancery Division (see Bankruptcy Rules 1952, S.I. 1952, No. 2113, rule 132, as amended by S.I. 1982, No. 1437).

[53]   Insolvency Rules 1986, r. 7.49. The nature of the appeal to the single judge under the new provisions has been held to be "a true appeal" and not a rehearing *de novo*: *Re Gilmartin (A Bankrupt)* [1989] 1 W.L.R. 513.

19.1   Section 15 of this paper summarised our proposals for reform of the procedure for judicial review. We now summarise the issues relevant to reform of the statutory provisions for appeals and applications to the High Court.

19.2   We have illustrated the variety of forms of applications to quash, statutory appeals and cases stated from the decisions of inferior courts and tribunals to the High Court, and sought to give some picture of the different purposes which they serve. The impact on the statute book of such a proliferation of provisions is obvious and the procedural complications for those bringing appeals before the High Court are considerable.

19.3   The aims of the Law Commission include the reduction of separate enactments and generally the simplification and modernisation of the law. There is a well justified and long established need for a statutory avenue of appeal to obtain a judicial determination on matters which have been the subject of consideration by an inferior tribunal or body. But is the proliferation of procedures justified? If not, reform should aim to prevent further proliferation of statutory provisions and to rationalise the various formulations in existing statutes, rules and High Court practice. This would not only clarify the purpose of the High Court's jurisdiction in this appellate, supervisory and reviewing field, but also provide clearer guidance to practitioners as to the procedures to be followed. We now summarise preliminary ideas for reform which arise out of our survey of this branch of the law. As indicated, we invite comment on the extent to which it is felt rationalisation is in principle desirable and possible. If it is, we also invite views as to how best to proceed. We canvass several possibilities. Whichever is favoured, if there is to be any rationalisation, we believe that it is desirable to use the expertise of the Council on Tribunals, whether in co-operation with the Commission or any other body.

Substantive Issues

The High Court's appellate jurisdiction

19.4   The views of consultees are invited on the following questions.

         19.4.1   Is it possible to state the criteria relevant to determining whether more than one judge should sit on a particular type of appeal?

         19.4.2   Is the constitution of the court a matter which should be left to judicial administration? Does it need to be clarified in primary legislation?

19.4.3 What interlocutory appellate matters can be dealt with by a Master (or District Judge of the Family Division)? Are the provisions in all the High Court divisions for dealing with interlocutory matters sufficiently clear and consistent?

Systematisation of forms of appeals, case stated and applications to quash

19.5 Reform may be needed to introduce appeal procedures which more clearly identify the purpose for which the appeal rights to the High Court have been granted, the issues under appeal and the powers that the Court is called on to or can employ on hearing such appeals.

19.6 We have drawn attention to the similarity in the way applications to quash are formulated. Could these be formulated in or by reference to one co-ordinated provision? What features of individual contexts would it be desirable to preserve?

19.7 Could all the existing forms of statutory appeal and application be simplified to two procedures:

19.7.1 firstly, powers of appeal or reference, whether by the tribunal or party, to the High Court on a point of law (including jurisdiction, legality and procedural propriety) and

19.7.2 secondly, appeals not limited to a point of law.

19.8 We invite views on the implications of the decision in *Chief Adjudication Officer* v. *Foster*,[1] and in particular whether there is a need to provide that the power to refer a question of law as to the validity of delegated legislation should enable the High Court to grant a supervisory remedy by way of judicial review.

Standing

19.9 We have discussed the broader policy considerations surrounding the issue of standing in judicial review in Part A.[2] Many statutes refer to a category of "persons aggrieved" as having the right to appeal, whilst others identify the category of potential appellants more precisely.[3] Some provisions give the decision-making body involved a special right, beside those of any other category of potential appellants, to

---

[1]   See above, para. 18.33.

[2]   See section 9.

[3]   We cite several examples of these different formulations in Annex 3.

refer a point of law to the High Court.[4] Reference may also be made to third parties who may have standing to intervene in an appeal, though not to make the appeal themselves.[5]

19.10 Where the formulation of standing is left in its most general form, courts have held that the category of "persons aggrieved" is wider than those whose legal rights have been affected by the decision.[6] A liberal approach was endorsed by the House of Lords in *Arsenal F.C.* v. *Ende*,[7] where it was held that a ratepayer was within the class of persons aggrieved even where he had not suffered personal financial or other loss from an alleged under-assessment of rates on land in his Borough. In another case it was held that a "person aggrieved" included any party to proceedings where the decision was adverse to her or him.[8]

19.11 The relationship between the test for "persons aggrieved" in statutory appeals and the test for "sufficient interest" in judicial review proceedings is unclear. In the *National Federation of Self-Employed*[9] Lord Diplock suggested that the words "sufficient interest" were deliberately avoided in the drafting of R.S.C. Order 53 to give the court a wider discretion by avoiding the gloss placed by existing case law on the term "any person aggrieved". However, the fusion of merits and discretion in the criteria for standing in judicial review since the *National Federation of Self-Employed* case, may in practice have made the requirements stricter than those for "any person aggrieved" in statutory appeals. On the other hand, it has been said[10] that the courts are equating the test for "any person aggrieved" with that of "sufficient interest". In any event, the trend towards specifying in more detail those with rights of appeal may

---

[4] Planning (Listed Buildings and Conservation Areas) Act 1990, s.65; Town and Country Planning Act 1990, s.288; Copyright, Designs and Patents Act 1988, s.251.

[5] We comment below, at paras. 19.26 and 27 on the issues concerning those directly affected by decisions, who may wish to intervene.

[6] *Attorney-General of the Gambia v. N'jie* [1961] A.C. 617, 634.

[7] [1979] A.C. 1.

[8] *Cook* v. *Southend B.C.* [1990] 2 Q.B. 1.

[9] [1982] A.C. 617, 642, where Lord Diplock suggested that the sufficient interest test is wider than that for "aggrieved persons".

[10] *Cook* v. *Southend B.C.* [1990] 2 Q.B. 1, 18. See also R.J.F. Gordon, *Crown Office Proceedings* (1990), G1-013, P. Cane, *An Introduction of Administrative Law* (2nd ed., 1992) p 49, n. 16; and C.T. Emery and B. Smythe, *Judicial Review: Legal Limits of Official Power* (1986), p.312, though the case referred to in the latter text (*Arsenal F.C.* v. *Ende*) does not explicitly discuss any similarity between these two terms.

have the effect of reducing the similarities between the tests of standing applicable to statutory appeals and in judicial review.

19.12 We seek views on whether, where statutory appeals only refer to standing in general terms, such as "person aggrieved", it is desirable for that term to differ from the general formulation used in judicial review.

Time limits

19.13 The general provision[11] for appeals is that the appeal notice must be served within 28 days. In the case of statutory review, the most common period fixed on is six weeks. We would invite views on whether the differences in time limits are necessary or justified, given the apparent benefits of having one, rather than a variety of, time limits governing the appellate jurisdiction. Could the provisions for statutory appeals and statutory review agree upon the same time period for appeals and, if so, what should it be?

19.14 The manner of computation of the time period, where it runs from the date of notification of a decision to the would-be appellant, has been questioned,[12] and the matter could be put more clearly by deciding whether the date of receipt of a decision letter or statement of reasons by the appellant is to be the starting point for the computation of time.

Power to extend time

19.15 We have commented earlier on the differences in the extent to which the court, exercising its statutory jurisdiction, has power to extend time for appealing. Are these differences defensible: should the court have the power to extend time for statutory review cases,[13] or should there be an absolute bar on extending time for all appeals?

---

[11]   R.S.C., O. 55, r.4(2).

[12]   Gordon, *op. cit.* refers to the different views taken in *Minister of Labour* v. *Genner Iron & Steel Co. (Wollescote) Ltd.* [1967] 1 W.L.R. 1386, and *Griffiths* v. *Secretary of State for the Environment* [1983] 2 A.C. 51.

[13]   As in the case of fraud or bad faith, on which see *R.* v. *Secretary of State for the Environment, ex p. Ostler* [1977] Q.B. 122, para. 17.4 above.

Interim suspension and stay of orders pending appeal

19.16 As mentioned above[14] this is an area in respect of which there is considerable difference between the various procedures. Are the present provisions as to stay or suspension of orders appropriate, and could they be harmonised? Should the presumption be for suspension of disputed orders or that they remain in force unless the court orders to the contrary?

19.17 There are other interlocutory applications which may be made, including for example, applications for security for costs of the appeal. Is it possible to provide further clarification as to which interlocutory applications can or cannot be made within the appellate jurisdiction of the High Court?

The orders which can be made on appeal

19.18 Individual statutes usually make express provision as to the orders which the High Court may make on appeal, thereby indicating the extent to which control over the decisions of an inferior court, tribunal or other body is being subjected to appeal or review by the High Court. Views are invited as to whether the scope of the High Court's powers on appeal might be clarified if the High Court's order-making powers on appeals and applications were set out in an appeals provision of general effect.

Rights of appeal to the High Court

19.19 Rights of access to the courts raise issues as to whether rights of appeal etc. are to be as of right or subject to a leave requirement. Case stated provides a further variation in enabling the tribunal to refuse to state a case if it does not think that a point of law is in issue, and empowering the High Court, if it thinks fit, to require the tribunal to do so. Views are invited as to what principles should govern the right to appeal, or the grant of leave, in relation to the different procedures which have been reviewed in this part of the paper.

Relationship between appeals and judicial review

19.20 In paragraph 2.15 of this paper, we noted that many judicial review applications are initiated as desperate and ill-disguised attempts to appeal against the decision in question. Views are invited as to whether the distinctions between those cases where

---

[14] See paras. 17.3 and 18.3 above. The picture is further complicated where the regulations governing the particular tribunal deal with this obliquely in provisions detailing how and when the final determination is to be notified to the relevant parties.

a right of appeal to the High Court exists[15] and those where they do not are legally defensible in terms of principle.

19.21 We also invite views as to whether the relationship between judicial review and the various statutory appellate mechanisms has caused difficulties, either in general or in a particular area. One way in which this can occur is where statutory rights of appeal do not empower an appellate body to consider public law issues such as the vires of regulations,[16] procedural irregularity, or *Wednesbury* unreasonableness.[17] We invite views as to the respective advantages and disadvantages of accepting some overlap between appellate and reviewing bodies as there has been in the case of appeal on a point of law. Will restricting appellate bodies from considering some or all public law issues lead to a new and undesirable procedural dichotomy and what impact will it have on the rule, discussed in section 14,[18] that, in general, alternative remedies, such as statutory remedies, must be exhausted before resorting to judicial review?

Procedural Issues

19.22 As regards rationalisation of the procedures governed by rules of court, we seek views on the following issues.

19.22.1 Are the rules governing the way in which appeals are presented so phrased as to ensure that the parties know what is required?

19.22.2 Do the appeal papers lodged provide the High Court with all the necessary information as to the factual and legal background to the dispute, the adjudication before the inferior tribunal, the evidence, the relevant contentions as to points of law (or fact), the issues requiring determination, and the order sought on appeal?

19.22.3 Are there improvements to the appeals procedure which would be more effective in enabling the appeal to come on for adjudication with the minimum of delay and cost?

19.22.4 Is there a need for more explicit coverage of the interlocutory steps necessary before an appeal can come on for full hearing, or would this encourage unnecessary delay and costs?

---

[15]   Either directly or subject to proceedings in an inferior court or tribunal.

[16]   See paras. 18.33 - 18.35.

[17]   See paras. 14.10 and 18.10 above.

[18]   Paras. 14.6 - 14.15.

19.23 Rules of court give little help as to the different purposes served by the different forms of appeal. There is little in R.S.C., Orders 55 and 56 which identify significant differences between the forms of appeal that they cover. The rules might be arranged more clearly, perhaps by use of tables and clearer cross-referencing between rules of general relevance and those particular to appeals concerning parties, service, time limits, evidence, interim applications which are specifically relevant to appeals etc..

The form originating the appeal

19.24 Could all appeals be initiated by reference to the same originating appeal process? Could the Franks Committee's preference for straight appeals on a point of law replace case stated procedure entirely? In what form would the lower court's reasoning be stated?

19.25 We have commented earlier on the pros and cons for case stated procedure.[19] Is it possible to retain useful elements of the case stated procedure, whilst still advocating a single format for appeals to the High Court?

Respondents to appeals

19.26 Much space is devoted both in statute and in rules to identifying the correct respondent and other parties to be served. This approach is in contrast with the provisions for judicial review, which refers more generally, in R.S.C., Order 53, rule 5(3) to the requirement to serve the application on all persons directly affected, which taken in conjunction with rule 9(1) enables almost anyone with an interest in the subject matter to appear at the full hearing. It has been brought to our attention that the procedure used in judicial review may be more effective than that in statutory appeals. The present rules have, on occasion, precluded representations being made at the hearing of a statutory appeal, by the Government Department most closely concerned.[20]

19.27 Given that points of public importance may arise on statutory appeals as in judicial review, it would seem appropriate to have a similar test for those regarded by the court as a proper person to be heard (as in Order 53, rule 9(1)); a more restrictive test may prove counter-productive. Given the variety of bodies and tribunals from which appeals may stem, some elaboration is inevitable, but it is debatable whether the way in which this is presently covered in statutes, regulations and rules of court, is the best that can be devised. We invite comment on this point.

---

[19]   See paras. 18.13 -18.16 above.

[20]   *Harrison* v. *Cornwall County Council* (unreported: C.O. 475/91) (C.A.) Counsel's transcript, 25 July 1991. This case concerned an appeal from the Registered Home Tribunal under the Registered Homes Act 1984.

Entering the appeal

19.28   Many but not all appeals are channelled through the Crown Office. Are there differences in the administration of the offices serving the three Divisions which identify unnecessary inefficiencies and differences in the administrative aspects of handling such appeals?

Evidence on appeals

19.29   Despite the absence of express requirements concerning filing of affidavits, it is in practice desirable on appeals that the appellant should file affidavit evidence exhibiting the decision appealed from and setting out the general context.[21] Given that the appeal notice must state why the decision impugned is wrong,[22] it would seem beneficial for the High Court and the respondents to see such affidavit evidence at the same time as the appeal notice. Are there any reasons why this should not be a provision of general effect?

The hearing

19.30   The misleading appellation of "appeals by way of rehearing" has been commented on. It must be counter-productive for rules to place such false emphases. We invite views as to the scope for eliminating confusing differences in appeal procedures, and for promoting greater clarity as to the procedure to be adopted at the appeal hearing.

Further Appeals

19.31   The provisions governing appeals from the High Court's decision on appeals also require consideration. What principles should govern the possibility of further appeals from the High Court's determination of an appeal from a lower court or decision maker?

19.32   Views are also welcome on the current provisions for appeals to magistrates' courts and county courts (and certain provisions which allow appeals which would otherwise go to the High Court to leapfrog to the Court of Appeal) from the decisions of tribunals and other bodies. Reform of appeal procedures to the High Court will have a consequential effect on these appeals.

---

21   Gordon, *op. cit.*, E2-008.

22   The Supreme Court Practice 1993, vol. 1, para. 55/3/2.

19.33 We have commented on the developing trend of assigning jurisdiction between levels of adjudicator on the basis of difficulty.[23] Views are invited as to whether reform of the provisions for appeals to the High Court might have the side effect of hindering or facilitating that trend.

How to proceed?

19.34 If there is support for the principle of rationalisation, the question arises of how to proceed. There are a number of possibilities.

(a) To make detailed proposals for a series of procedures which, although suitable for the majority of contexts, would take account of the particular requirements of an individual context.

(b) To make detailed proposals for those procedures which are handled by the Crown Office, subject again to the need to reflect the particular requirements of an individual context.

(c) That a number of model procedures could be developed which would be available when new procedures are being developed or when changes to existing procedures are being considered. Specific contexts would be able to adopt the appropriate model or models either with or without individual variations to reflect their particular needs. Even if there were a considerable number of such variations, the overall effect in the long term might be simplification and rationalisation.

If there is support for the principle of rationalisation, we invite views as to the relative merits of these possibilities, or of any alternative.

---

[23]   e.g. most recently under Orders made pursuant to the Courts and Legal Services Act 1990, but also in relation to charities, patents, insolvency and other areas referred to earlier, see para. 18.30 above.

ANNEX 1

SECTION 31 OF THE SUPREME COURT ACT 1981

31.- (1) An application to the High Court for one or more of the following forms of relief, namely -

(a) an order of mandamus, prohibition or certiorari;

(b) a declaration or injunction under subsection (2); or

(c) an injunction under section 30 restraining a person not entitled to do so from acting in an office to which that section applies,

shall be made in accordance with rules of court by a procedure to be known as an application for judicial review.

(2) A declaration may be made or an injunction granted under this subsection in any case where an application for judicial review, seeking that relief, has been made and the High Court considers that, having regard to -

(a) the nature of the matters in respect of which relief may be granted by orders of mandamus, prohibition or certiorari;

(b) the nature of the persons and bodies against whom relief may be granted by such orders; and

(c) all the circumstances of the case,

it would be just and convenient for the declaration to be made or the injunction to be granted, as the case may be.

(3) No application for judicial review shall be made unless the leave of the High Court has been obtained in accordance with rules of court; and the court shall not grant leave to make such an application unless it consider that the applicant has a sufficient interest in the matter to which the application relates.

(4) On an application for judicial review the High Court may award damages to the applicant if -

(a) he has joined with his application a claim for damages arising from any matter to which the application relates; and

(b) the court is satisfied that, if the claim had been made in an action begun by the applicant at the time of making his application, he would have been awarded damages.

(5) If, on an application for judicial review seeking an order of certiorari, the High Court quashes the decision to which the application relates, the High Court may remit the matter to the court, tribunal or authority concerned, with a direction to reconsider it and reach a decision in accordance with the findings of the High Court.

(6) Where the High Court considers that there has been undue delay in making an application for judicial review, the court may refuse to grant -

(a) leave for the making of the application; or

(b) any relief sought on the application,

if it considers that the granting of the relief sought would be likely to cause substantial hardship to, or substantially prejudice the rights of, any person or would be detrimental to good administration.

(7) Subsection (6) is without prejudice to any enactment or rule of court which has the effect of limiting the time within which an application for judicial review may be made."

116

R.S.C. ORDER 53

APPLICATIONS FOR JUDICIAL REVIEW

Cases appropriate for application for judicial review

1.-   (1)   An application for-

        (a)   an order of mandamus, prohibition or certiorari, or
        (b)   an injunction under section 30 of the Act restraining a person from acting in any office in which he is not entitled to act,

shall be made by way of an application for judicial review in accordance with the provisions of this Order.

    (2)   An application for a declaration or an injunction (not being an injunction mentioned in paragraph (1)(b)) may be made by way of an application for judicial review, and on such an application the Court may grant the declaration or injunction claimed if it consider that, having regard to -

        (a)   the nature of the matters in respect of which relief may be granted by way of an order of mandamus, prohibition or certiorari,

        (b)   the nature of the persons and bodies against whom relief may be granted by way of such an order, and

        (c)   all the circumstances of the case,

it would be just and convenient for the declaration or injunction to be granted on an application for judicial review.

Joinder of claims for relief

2.   On an application for judicial review any relief mentioned in rule 1(1) or (2) may be claimed as an alternative or in addition to any other relief so mentioned if it arises out of or relates to or is connected with the same matter.

Grant of leave to apply for judicial review

3.-   (1)   No application for judicial review shall be made unless the leave of the Court has been obtained in accordance with this rule.

    (2)   An application for leave must be made *ex parte* to a judge by filing in the Crown Office -

        (a)   a notice in Form No. 86A containing a statement of

            (i)   the name and description of the applicant,

            (ii)   the relief sought and the grounds upon which it is sought,

            (iii)   the name and address of the applicant's solicitors (if any) and

            (iv)   the applicant's address for service; and

        (b)   an affidavit which verifies the facts relied on.

    (3)   The judge may determine the application without a hearing, unless a hearing is requested in the notice of application, and need not sit in open court; in any case, the Crown Office shall serve a copy of the judge's order on the applicant.

(4)   Where the application for leave is refused by the judge, or is granted on terms, the applicant may renew it by applying -

(a)   in any criminal cause or matter, to a Divisional Court of the Queen's Bench Division;

(b)   in any other case, to a single judge sitting in open court or, if the Court so directs, to a Divisional Court of the Queen's Bench Division:

Provided that no application for leave may be renewed in any non-criminal cause or matter in which the judge has refused leave under paragraph (3) after a hearing.

(5)   In order to renew his application for leave the applicant must, within 10 days of being served with notice of the judge's refusal, lodge in the Crown Office notice of his intention in Form No. 86B.

(6)   Without prejudice to its powers under Order 20, rule 8, the Court hearing an application for leave may allow the applicant's statement to be amended, whether by specifying different grounds of relief or otherwise, on such terms, if any, as it thinks fit.

(7)   The Court shall not grant leave unless it considers that the applicant has a sufficient interest in the matter to which the application relates.

(8)   Where leave is sought to apply for an order of certiorari to remove for the purpose of its being quashed any judgment, order conviction or other proceedings which is subject to appeal and a time is limited for the bringing of the appeal, the Court may adjourn the application for leave until the appeal is determined or the time for appealing has expired.

(9)   If the Court grants leave, it may impose such terms as to costs and as to giving security as it thinks fit.

(10)   Where leave to apply for judicial review is granted, then -

(a)   if the relief sought is an order of prohibition or certiorari and the Court so directs, the grant shall operate as a stay of the proceedings to which the application relates until the determination of the application or until the Court otherwise orders;

(b)   if any other relief is sought, the Court may at any time grant in the proceedings such interim relief as could be granted in an action begun by writ.

Delay in applying for relief

4.-   (1)   An application for leave to apply for judicial review shall be made promptly and in any event within three months from the date when grounds for the application first arose unless the Court considers that there is good reason for extending the period within which the application shall be made.

(2)   Where the relief sought is an order of certiorari in respect of any judgment, order, conviction or other proceeding, the date when grounds for the application first arose shall be taken to be the date of that judgment, order, conviction or proceeding.

(3)   The preceding paragraphs are without prejudice to any statutory provision which has the effect of limiting the time within which an application for judicial review may be made.

Mode of applying for judicial review

5.-   (1)   In any criminal cause or matter, where leave has been granted to make an application for judicial review, the application shall be made by originating motion to a Divisional Court of the Queen's Bench Division.

(2)   In any other such cause or matter, where leave has been granted to make an application for judicial review, the application shall be made by originating motion to a judge sitting in open court, unless the Court directs that it shall be made -

(a)   by originating summons to a judge in chambers; or

118

(b)   by originating motion to a Divisional Court of the Queen's Bench Division.

Any direction under sub-paragraph (a) shall be without prejudice to the judge's powers under Order 32, rule 13.

(3)   The notice of motion or summons must be served on all persons directly affected and where it relates to any proceedings in or before a court and the object of the application is either to compel the court or an officer of the court to do any act in relation to the proceedings or to quash them or any order made therein, the notice or summons must also be served on the clerk or registrar of the court and, where any objection to the conduct of the judge is to be made, on the judge.

(4)   Unless the Court granting leave has otherwise directed, there must be at least 10 days between the service of the notice of motion or summons and the hearing.

(5)   A motion must be entered for hearing within 14 days after the grant of leave.

(6)   An affidavit giving the names and addresses of, and the places and dates of service on, all persons who have been served with the notice of motion or summons must be filed before the summons is entered for hearing and, if any person who ought to be served under this rule has not been served, the affidavit must state that fact and the reason for it; and the affidavit shall be before the Court on the hearing of the motion or summons.

(7)   If on the hearing of the motion or summons the Court is of opinion that any person who ought, whether under this rule or otherwise, to have been served has not been served, the Court may adjourn the hearing on such terms (if any) as it may direct in order that the notice or summons may be served on that person.

Statements and affidavits

6.-   (1)   Copies of the statement in support of an application for leave under rule 3 must be served with the notice of motion or summons and, subject to paragraph (2), no grounds shall be relied upon or any relief sought at the hearing except the grounds and relief set out in the statement.

(2)   The Court may on the hearing of the motion or summons allow the applicant to amend his statement, whether by specifying different or additional grounds or relief or otherwise, on such terms, if any, as it thinks fit and may allow further affidavits to be used if they deal with new matters arising out of an affidavit of any other party to the application.

(3)   Where the applicant intends to ask to be allowed to amend his statement or to use further affidavits, he shall give notice of his intention and of any proposed amendment to every other party.

(4)   Any respondent who intends to use an affidavit at the hearing shall file it in the Crown Office as soon as practicable and in any event, unless the Court otherwise directs, within 56 days after service upon him of the documents required to be served by paragraph (1).

(5)   Each party to the application must supply to every other party on demand and on payment of the proper charges copies of every affidavit which he proposes to use at the hearing, including, in the case of the applicant, the affidavit in support of the application for leave under rule 3.

Claim for damages

7.-   (1)   On an application for judicial review the Court may, subject to paragraph (2), award damages to the applicant if -

(a)   he has included in the statement in support of his application for leave under rule 3 a claim for damages arising from any matter to which the application relates, and

(b)   the Court is satisfied that, if the claim had been made in an action begun by the applicant at the time of making his application, he could have been awarded damages.

(2)   Order 18, rule 12, shall apply to a statement relating to a claim for damages as it applies to a pleading.

Application for discovery, interrogatories, cross-examination etc

8.-   (1)   Unless the Court otherwise directs, any interlocutory application in proceedings on an application for judicial review may be made to a judge or a master of the Queen's Bench Division, notwithstanding that the application for judicial review has been made by motion and is to be heard by a Divisional Court.

In this paragraph "interlocutory application" includes an application for an order under Order 24 or 26 or Order 38, rule 2(3) or for an order dismissing the proceedings by consent of the parties.

(2)   In relation to an order made by a master pursuant to paragraph (1) Order 58, rule 1, shall, where the application for judicial review is to be heard by a Divisional Court, have effect as if a reference to that Court were substituted for the reference to a judge in chambers.

(3)   This rule is without prejudice to any statutory provision or rule of law restricting the making of an order against the Crown.

Hearing of application for judicial review

9.-   (1)   On the hearing of any motion or summons under rule 5, any person who desires to be heard in opposition to the motion or summons, and appears to the Court to be a proper person to be heard, shall be heard, notwithstanding that he has not been served with notice of the motion or the summons.

(2)   Where the relief sought is or includes an order of certiorari to remove any proceedings for the purpose of quashing them, the applicant may not question the validity of any order, warrant, commitment, conviction, inquisition or record unless before the hearing of the motion or summons he has lodged in the Crown Office a copy thereof verified by affidavit or accounts for his failure to do so to the satisfaction of the Court hearing the motion or summons.

(3)   Where an order for certiorari is made in any such case as is referred to in paragraph (2) the order shall, subject to paragraph (4) direct that the proceedings shall be quashed forthwith on their removal into the Queen's Bench Division.

(4)   Where the relief sought is an order of certiorari and the Court is satisfied that there are grounds for quashing the decision to which the application relates, the Court may, in addition to quashing it, remit the matter to the court, tribunal or authority concerned with a direction to reconsider it and reach a decision in accordance with the findings of the Court.

(5)   Where the relief sought is a declaration, an injunction or damages and the Court consider that it should not be granted on an application for judicial review but might have been granted if it had been sought in an action begun by writ by the applicant at the time of making his application, the Court may, instead of refusing the application, order the proceedings to continue as if they had been begun by writ; and Order 28, rule 8, shall apply as if, in the case of an application made by motion, it had been made by summons.

... (rules 10, 11, 12, not reproduced here)

Appeal from judge's order

13.   No appeal shall lie from an order made under paragraph (3) of rule 3 on an application for leave which may be renewed under paragraph (4) of that rule.

Meaning of Court

14.   In relation to the hearing by a judge of an application for leave under rule 3 or of an application for judicial review, any reference in this Order to "the Court" shall, unless the context otherwise requires, be construed as a reference to the judge."

ANNEX 2

LIST OF CURRENT STATUTORY PROVISIONS FOR APPEALS ETC
TO THE HIGH COURT

PART A: PRIMARY LEGISLATION[1]

1992

Tribunals and Inquiries Act 1992 c.53,

s.11,   (any party to proceedings before certain tribunals if dissatisfied in point of law with a decision of the tribunal may either appeal from the tribunal or require the tribunal to state a case).

Friendly Societies Act 1992 c.40,

s.61   (appeal on a point of law from any decision of the tribunal under s.59 by a friendly society or other person concerned or by the Commission).

Social Security Administration Act 1992 c.5,

s.18   (appeal by any person aggrieved by the refusal of the Secretary of State to refer a question of law to the High Court);

s.58   (regulations as to determination of questions and matters arising out of pending reviews and appeals).

1991

Land Drainage Act 1991 c.59,

sch.3   (statutory review of unconfirmed orders).

Statutory Water Companies Act 1991 c.58,

s.5   (appeals in respect of applications under s.4);

s.12   (review of a special resolution in relation to a company adoption of memorandum and articles).

Water Resources Act 1991 c.57,

s.69   (statutory review to challenge validity of decisions of Secretary of State and related proceedings);

sch.3   (statutory review to challenge a s.108 order);

sch.16   (statutory review of unconfirmed orders imposing special drainage charges).

---

[1]   In force 1 September 1992.

Water Industry Act 1991 c.56,

s.137   (Director General of Water Services may state a case on a question of law arising from appeals under ss.122 or 126(1) of the Act).

s.45   (Lord Chancellor may make provisions for appeal to the High Court instead of the Child Support Appeal Tribunal).

1990

Courts and Legal Services Act 1990 c.41,

s.42   (appeal by a person aggrieved by a decision of the Conveyancing Appeal Tribunal, or at the instance of the Board, on any question of law arising from that decision);

sch.7   (a practitioner may request that the Conveyancing Ombudsman state a case on any question of law).

Human Fertilisation and Embryology Act 1990 c.37,

s.21   (appeal against the decision of the H.F.E.A. to refuse, vary or revoke a licence under s.20 on a point of law).

Planning (Hazardous Substances) Act 1990 c.10,

s.22   (statutory review).

Planning (Listed Buildings and Conservation Areas) Act 1990 c.9,

s.65 and sch.3 (appeals relating to listed building enforcement notices).

Town and Country Planning Act 1990 c.8,

s.288   (statutory review: proceedings for questioning the validity of certain orders, decisions and directions);

s.289   (appeals relating to enforcement notices issued under s.207. This section was amended by sec.6 Planning and Compensation Act 1991 c.34 so that the leave of the High Court is now required before the appeal can be brought);

sch. 15(7)   (appeals against compliance determinations or failure to make such determinations).

1989

Children Act 1989 c.41,

s.94   (appeal from an order of a magistrate).

Extradition Act 1989 c.33,

s.10   (court of committal may be required to state a case).

1988

Copyright, Designs and Patents Act 1988 c.48,

s.152   (appeals on a point of law from Copyright Tribunal);
s.251   (references and appeals on design right matters);
s.300   (appeal relating to disposal of offending articles).

Coroners Act 1988 c.13,

s.13   (power of High Court to quash verdict).

Criminal Justice Act 1988 c.33,

s.113   (right of appeal on question of law from determination of Criminal Injuries Compensation Board).

Local Government Finance Act 1988 c.41,

sch.11   (appeal from decision or order of a tribunal on an appeal under s.23).

1987

Banking Act 1987 c.22,

s.31   (further appeals on points of law from a decision of a tribunal on an appeal under s.27).

Coal Industry Act 1987 c.3,

s.8   (statutory review of Secretary of State's orders in relation to social welfare bodies and superannuation schemes).

Petroleum Act 1987 c.12,

s.14   (statutory review).

1986

Airports Act 1986 c.31,

s.49   (statutory review).

Building Societies Act 1986 c.53,

s.39   (appeal against a determination of the Building Society Commission);
s.49   (further appeals on points of law);
s.84   (adjudicator under a recognised scheme may be requested to state a case).

Insolvency Act 1986 c.45,

s.375   (appeal from a decision of a county court or from a registrar in bankruptcy to the High Court).

Administration of Justice Act 1985 c.61,

s.26(8)
and sch.4   (appeal against order made by the licensed conveyers to the Discipline and Appeals Committee).

Housing Associations Act 1985 c.69,

s.7   (appeals by any body aggrieved by a decision of the Housing Corporation to remove it from the register);
s.16   (appeals against removal of committee member);
s.30   (appeals against removal of a member for misconduct).

Films Act 1985 c.21,

sch.1(9)   (appeal against Secretary of State's decision).

Transport Act 1985 c.67,

s.9   (appeal on a point of law arising from a decision of the Secretary of State in an appeal under section 7);
s.43   (appeal on a point of law arising from a decision of the Secretary of State on an appeal of the Metropolitan Traffic Commissioner).

Finance Act 1985 c.54,

s.26(2)   (Lord Chancellor may provide for an appeal from a V.A.T. tribunal).

Building Act 1984 c.55,

s.42   (appeal and statement of case to High Court in certain cases).

Cycle Tracks Act 1984 c.38,

s.3(8)   (statutory review).

Data Protection Act 1984 c.35,

s.14(5)   (appeal from the Data Protection Tribunal by any party to the tribunal proceedings).

Dentists Act 1984 c.25,

s. 30(6)   (appeal against suspension of registration).

Inheritance Tax Act 1984 c.51,

s.222   (appeal against notice of determination of the Commissioners of Inland Revenue);
s.225   (appeal from determination of Special Commissioners who may be requested to state a case).

Telecommunications Act 1984 c.12,

s.18   (statutory review).

1983

Mental Health Act 1983 c.20,

s.78(8)   (Mental Health Tribunal may state a case).

Representation of the People Act 1983 c.2,

s.146   (special case for determination of High Court).

Medical Act 1983 c.54,

s.38(6)   (application to terminate any suspension of a person registered in the medical register).

Pilotage Act 1983 c.21,

s.23   (further appeal from the decision of a magistrates' court on a question of law and fact)

1982

Civil Aviation Act 1982 c.16,

sch.7(7)   (statutory review).

Local Government and Finance Act 1982 c.32,

s.20   (appeal from decision of auditor who has stated his or her reasons in writing);
s.25   (auditor may make an application for judicial review of acts of a body which has been audited).

1981

Acquisition of Land Act 1981 c.67,

s.23   (statutory review by person aggrieved by a compulsory purchase order).

Animal Health Act 1981 c.22,

sch.1(3)   (appeal by a person aggrieved by the revocation or suspension of his or her licence to manufacture certain items).

Betting and Gaming Duties Act 1981 c.63,

sch.3(15)   (appeal for declaration of correct duty payable).

New Towns Act 1981 c.64,

sch.1   (statutory review of designation orders).

125

Supreme Court Act 1981 c.54,

s.28   (appeals from Crown Courts and inferior courts)

Wildlife and Countryside Act 1981 c.69,

sch.11   (statutory review).

1980

Highways Act 1980 c.66,

sch.2(2)   (statutory review of the validity of a scheme or order).

Local Government, Planning and Land Act 1980 c.65,

sch.32(4)   (statutory review to challenge the validity of enterprise zone scheme).

Magistrates' Courts Act 1980 c.43,

s.111   (application to magistrates to state a case).

1979

Ancient Monuments and Archaeological Areas Act 1979 c.46,

s.55   (statutory review).

Arbitration Act 1979 c.42,

s.1(1)   (High Court has jurisdiction to set aside or remit an award on the grounds of errors of fact or law on the face of the record);
s.1(2)   (appeal on any question of law arising out of an arbitration award).

Estate Agents Act 1979 c.38,

s.7   (appeal on a point of law from a decision of the Secretary of State).

1978

Domestic Proceedings and Magistrates' Courts Act 1978 c.22,

s.29   (appeal where a magistrates' court makes or refuses to make, varies or refuses to vary, revokes or refuses to revoke an order).

1977

Patents Act 1977 c.37,

s.97   (appeal to the Patents Court from any decision of the Comptroller).

Development of Rural Wales 1976 c.75,

sch.3(25)   (statutory review).

Adoption Act 1976 c.36,

s.63   (appeal from magistrates' court).

Farriers (Registration) Act 1975 c.35,

s.15(3)   (appeal against removal of name from register).

Friendly Societies Act 1974 c.46,

s.16   (appeal from refusal to register);
s.20   (appeal from refusal to register amendment of rule);
s.78   (statement of case and discovery);
s.83(7)   (objections to amalgamation and transfers of engagements of friendly societies);
s.92   (appeals against cancellation of registration and suspension of business).

Solicitors Act 1974 c. 47,

s.13   (appeal against Society's failure to issue practising certificate);
s.49   (appeal from Solicitors' Disciplinary Tribunal);
s.50   (jurisdiction of Supreme Court over solicitors).

Social Security Act 1973 c.38 ,

s.86   (references and appeals from the two Boards).

Superannuation Act 1972 c.11,

s.2(7)   (case stated on question of law relating to civil service pension schemes);
s.11   (case stated relating to local government, health service and teachers' superannuation schemes).

1970

Taxes Management Act 1970 c.9,

s.53   (appeal against penalty imposed by Special Commissioners);
s.56   (the Commissioners may be required to state a case);
s.100C   (penalty proceedings against Commissioners).

Merchant Shipping Act 1970 c.36,

s.57/s.58   (power of Board of Trade to order rehearing by High Court of inquiry about shipping casualties).

1969

Transport (London) Act 1969 c.35,

s.23B (appeal on point of law from Minister's decision concerning authorisation of bus service).

1968

Medicines Act 1968 c.35,

s.82   (appeal against disqualification by Statutory Committee);
s.83   (appeal against refusal to revoke disqualification).

Hearing Aid Council Act 1968 c.50,

s.9   (appeal from Disciplinary Committee's decision to erase of a name from register).

1967

Agriculture Act 1967 c.22,

s.21   (appeal relating to documents required for inquiries by Meat and Livestock Commission);
s.49(5)   (appeal relating to purchase of land in Rural Development Board Area);
sch.2   (statutory review).

Forestry Act 1967 c.10,

sch 5(7)   (statutory review to challenge compulsory purchase order).

1965

Commons Registration Act 1965 c.64,

s.18   (appeal by any person aggrieved by a decision of the Commons Commissioners).

Nuclear Installations Act 1965 c.57,

s.16   (appeals over claims for compensation).

Industrial and Provident Societies Act 1965 c.12,

s.9   (appeals from refusal, cancellation or suspension of registration of society by registrar);
s.60   (registrar may state case on question of law).

1963

Water Resources Act 1963 c.38,

s.117   (statutory review).

1962

Pipe-lines Act 1962 c.58,

sch.2   (statutory review by any person aggrieved to challenge a compulsory purchase order).

1961

Public Health Act 1961 c.64,

s.66   (appeal by way of case stated on a point of law from Minister's decision on appeal to the High Court).

Land Compensation Act 1961 c.33,

s.21   (statutory review).

1960

Charities Act 1960 c.58,

s.5   (appeals against decision of Charities Commissioners relating to the registration of charities);
s.18   (concurrent jurisdiction with High Court for certain purposes);
s.20(7)   (appeal against removal of charity's trustee);
s.42   (appeals from Commissioners and Minister).

1959

Obscene Publications Act 1959 c.66,

s.3(5)   (appeal by way of case stated against forfeiture of articles).

1958

Land Powers (Defence) Act 1958 c.30,

sch.2   (statutory review).

1955

Children and Young Persons (Harmful Publications) Act 1955 c.28,

s.3   (appeals by way of case stated against order for seizure of articles under the Act).

1954

Agriculture (Miscellaneous Provisions) Act 1954 c.28,

s.6   (power of Agricultural Land Tribunal to refer questions of law to High Court).

Mines and Quarries Act 1954 c.70,

s.165   (appeals to quash conviction under the Act by order of certiorari).

Pharmacy Act 1954 c.61,

s.10   (appeals from Statutory Committee relating to registration);
s.11   (order not effective until appeal determined).

1949

Coast Protection Act 1949 c.74,

sch.1(3)   (statutory review).

Registered Designs Act 1949 c.88

s.28   (High Court acts as Appeal Tribunal from decisions of Registrar).

1947

Crown Proceedings Act 1947 c.44,

s.35(3)   (special rules of court to govern appeals in revenue matters to the High Court).

1943

Pension Appeal Tribunals Act 1943 c.39,

s.4   (appeals from the Pensions Appeal Tribunal by appellant or the Minister).

1939

London Building (Amendment) Act 1939 (2 & 3 Geo. 6 c xcvii),

s.55   (statutory review);
s.116   (Tribunal may state case for opinion of High Court).

1931

Architects (Registration) Act 1931 c.33,

s.9   (appeals against removal of name from register or disqualification by Architects Registration Council).

1925

Land Registration Act 1925 c.21,

s.140   (Power of Registrar to state case for opinion of High Court).

1923

Industrial Assurance Act 1923 c.8,

s.7   (appeal by a society aggrieved by the refusal of a Commissioner to allow further time for a deposit);
s.17   (appeal from Commissioner's orders as to expenses of inspection);
s.18   (appeals relating to valuations).

1906

Public Trustee Act 1906 c.55,

s.10   (application by person aggrieved by an act or omission of the public trustee in relation to any trust).

1898

Benefices Act 1898 c.48,

s.3   (appeal from decision of bishop not to institute or admit a presentee to a benefice to be heard by judge of the Supreme Court and archbishop).

1894

Merchant Shipping Act 1894 c.60,

s.478   (appeal against refusal of Board of Trade to order rehearing).

1891

Stamp Act 1891 c.39,

s.13   (appeal by way of case stated against Commissioner's assessment).

1845

Inclosure Act 1845 c.118,

ss.39, 44   (appeal from Commissioner's decision on boundary disputes).

1821

Cinque Ports Act 1821 c.76,

ss.4,5   (appeals to High Court of Admiralty by persons dissatisfied with salvage awards).

PART B: SUBORDINATE LEGISLATION[2]

(in reverse chronological order)

Children (Allocation of Proceedings) (Appeals) Order 1991 S.I. 1991, No. 1801.

art.2   (appeals against district judge order to transfer proceedings to a magistrates' court).

Family Proceedings Rules 1991 S.I. 1991, No. 1247.

r.2.42   (application for a re-hearing)
r.4.22   (appeals)
r.7.28   (appeal from variation of order by a magistrates' court)
r.8.2   (appeals under Domestic Proceedings and Magistrates Courts' Act 1978).

High Court and County Courts Jurisdiction Order 1991, S.I. 1991, No. 724.

art.6   (applications under s.19 and appeals under s.20 of the Local Government Finance Act 1982 to be commenced in High Court).

Non-Domestic Rating (Alteration of Lists and Appeals) Regulations 1990, S.I. 1990, No. 582.

Copyright Tribunal Rules 1989 S.I. 1989, No. 1129.

r. 42 and Sch. 3, form 17

               (sets out rules of procedure, including rules as to notices of appeal and prescribed form for appeals on a point of law under s. 152).

Magistrates' Court (Extradition) Rules 1989, S.I. 1989, No. 1597.

Valuation and Community Charge Tribunals Regulations 1989 S.I. 1989, No. 439.

reg.32   (regulations relating to appeals on a point of law).

Church of England Pensions Regulations 1988, S.I. 1988, No. 2256.

reg.32(3)   (appeal on any of the specified issues (listed in reg. 32(1) to the High Court).

---

[2]   The provisions below were in force on 1 September 1992 but it has not been possible to make the list an exhaustive one beyond 1 January 1992.

Parish and Community Meetings (Polls) Rules 1987, S.I. 1987, No.1.

r.36   (appeal on any order of a county court for production of documents).

Stamp Duty Reserve Tax Regulations 1986, S.I. 1986, No. 1711.

r.100   (appeal by any party on a question of law).

Social Security (Adjudication) Regulations 1986, S.I. 1986, No. 2218.

reg.16   (statement of grounds by Secretary of State to be provided to enable person to determine
                whether there may be grounds for an appeal on a point of law).

Insolvency Rules 1986, S.I. 1986, No. 1925.

rr. 7.47-7.49

                (rules as to appeals relating to individual and corporate insolvency to High Court from county
                courts).

Local Elections (Parishes and Communities) Rules 1986, S.I. 1986, No. 2215.

r.47(4) & sch. 2

                (rules as to appeal to High Court from county court order as to production of documents).

The Control of Off-Street Parking (England and Wales) (Metropolitan Districts) Order 1986, S.I. 1986, No.
225.

Part III, para 18(2)

                (appeal from Secretary of State on appeal from decision of district council).

Crown Court Rules 1982, S.I. 1982, No. 1109

r. 26   (procedure in Crown Court dealing with application to state case for the opinion of the High
                Court).

Magistrates' Courts Rules 1981, S.I. 1981, No. 552.

r. 76   (application to state a case);
r. 77   (consideration of draft case).

Estate Agents (Appeals) Regulations 1981, S.I. 1981, No. 1518.

r. 18   (notice of directions disposing of appeal by Secretary of State informing person of existence of right of appeal on point of law).

National Health Service (Compensation for Premature Retirement) Regulations 1981, S.I. 1981, No. 1263.

reg.12   (determination of questions: power of Secretary of State to state a special case for the High Court's opinion at any stage in the course of proceedings before him).

Pensions Appeal Tribunals (England and Wales) Rules 1980, S.I. 1980, No. 1120

s.25-32   (appeals on a error of law with leave).

Pensions Appeal Tribunals (Posthumous Appeals) Order 1980, S.I. 1980, No.1082.

s.4   (designates person to pursue right of appeal to High Court).

Consumer Credit Licensing (Appeals) Regulations 1976, S.I. 1976, No.837.

reg. 18   (notice disposing of appeal must inform of right of appeal on a point of law).

Friendly Societies Regulations 1975, S.I. 1975, No. 205.

sch.1, form AE, (prescribed form notice before cancellation or suspension of registration).

Disused Mine and Quarry Tips (Prescribed Forms) Regulations 1969, S.I. 1969, No. 807

                  (prescribed forms explaining rights of appeals from local council's requirements as to remedial action regarding waste tip).

Commons Registration (Objections and Maps) Regulations 1968, S.I. 1968, No. 989.

sch. 1   (prescribed forms explaining procedure on reference to Commons Commissioners or High Court).

RULES OF THE SUPREME COURT

Rules of the Supreme Court (Revision) 1965, S.I. 1965, No. 1776, as printed complete with all subsequent amendments in *'The Supreme Court Practice 1993'*.

In addition to the references to Orders 55 and 56 referred to in the main text, reference to rights of appeal and the procedure are to be found in (R.S.C.):

Order 73:	r.2 (determination of any question of law arising in the course of a reference, under s. 2(1) of the Arbitration Act 1979. Rules 3 and 6 identify the appropriate judicial officer).
Order 74:	(applications and appeals under the Merchant Shipping Acts 1894 to 1979): rules 1 and 2(1) identify the correct court; other rules specify required appeal documents and notice to be given).
Order 90:	r.29 (appeals under the Matrimonial Proceedings (Magistrates' Courts) Act 1960).
Order 91:	assignment of revenue proceedings to Chancery Division.
Order 93:	applications and appeals to High Court under various Acts, assigned to Chancery Division.
Order 94:	applications and Appeals to High Court under various Acts: Queen's Bench Division, including r.14 (applications under s.13, Coroners Act 1988: power of High Court to order inquest on application or with authority of Attorney General).
Order 98:	Local Government Finance Act 1982.
Order 100:	Trade Marks Act 1938 and Trade Marks (Amendment) Act 1984 (Appeals from the Registrar).
Order 101:	Pensions Appeal Tribunals Act 1943 (appeals to the High Court (QBD) from Pensions Appeal Tribunal).
Order 104:	The Patents Acts 1949 to 1961 and 1977; Registered Designs Acts 1949 to 1971; Defence Contracts Act 1958. Appeals from the Registrar under the 1949 Act (as amended and reprinted in sch. 4 to the Copyright, Designs and Patents Act 1988) go to the Appeal Tribunal which consists of High Court judges, but, by virtue of s.28(9) such appeals are not deemed to be a proceeding in the High Court.
Order 106:	proceedings relating to solicitors.
Order 108:	proceedings relating to charities: the Charities Act 1960.
Order 111:	the Social Security Acts 1975 to 1986.

ANNEX 3

EXAMPLES OF STATUTORY APPEALS WHERE STANDING IS MORE SPECIFIC THAN 'ANY PERSON AGGRIEVED'

- **Airports Act 1986, s. 49(1).**

  "If an airport operator is aggrieved...."
  (Appeal to the High Court to challenge the validity of an order made under s. 48 by the Civil Aviation Authority)

- **Telecommunications Act 1984, s. 18(1)**

  "If the telecommunications operator is aggrieved...."
  Application to the High Court to question the validity of an order of compliance with licence conditions issued by the Director General of Telecommunications.

- **Human Fertilisation and Embryology Act 1990, s.21.**

  "...any person on whom notice of the determination was served may appeal to the High Court..., on a point of law."
  Appeal possible where the Human Fertilisation and Embryology authority refuses to vary or revoke a licence after an appeal under s. 20.

- **Solicitors Act 1974, s. 49(2).**

  "(1) An appeal from the tribunal shall lie -

     (b) ... to the High Court.

  (2) Subject to subsection (3), an appeal shall lie at the instance of the applicant or complainant or of the person with respect to whom the application was made."

- **Medicines Act 1968, s. 107.**

  "(2) ...the person to whom such a decision relates desires to question the validity of the decision...."
  Appeal to the High Court challenging the decision of the licensing authority under Part II of the Act or a Minister under s. 75.

- **Education Act 1981, s. 16(3).**

  "If a parent is aggrieved by a refusal of the authority to comply with a request [to amend or revoke a school attendance order made under subsection 2] he may refer the question to the Secretary of State...."

- **Foreign Compensation Act 1969, s. 3(2),(6).**

  "(2)...the Commission shall, if so required by a person mentioned in subsection (6) below who is aggrieved by any determination of the Commission on any question of law relating to the jurisdiction of the Commission..., state and sign a case for the decision of the Court of Appeal.

  (6) The persons who may make a request ... are the claimant and any person appointed by the Commission to represent the interests of any fund out of which the claim would, if allowed, be met."

Printed in the United Kingdom for HMSO
Dd294464 1/93 C20 G3397 10170